BECOMING
A
PSYCHOTHERAPIST

DIFFERENT SCHOOLS
OF
HUMAN PSYCHOLOGY
AND
PSYCHOTHERAPY

Dr. Khalid Sohail
Dr. Rizwan Ali

Published in 2016 by GREENZONE Publishing, a division of
Dr. Sohail MPC Ltd.
213 Byron Street South
Whitby, Ontario, Canada L1N4P7
T. 905-666-7253 F, 905-666-4397
Websites: www.greenzoneliving.ca
www.dr.sohail.com

**National Library of Canada Cataloguing in
Publication**
Sohail, K. (Khalid), 1952-
Ali, Rizwan, 1964-

ISBN 978-927874-15-8
1. Psychotherapy. 2. Psychology,
I. Title.

Textual Design	Deana Seymore
Cover Design	Shahid Shafiq Nusoft Technologies

Dedicated
To
Adriana Davis
And
All Other Students
Of
Human Psychology
And
Social Work
Psychiatry
And
Psychotherapy

Special thanks
to
Anne Henderson
for
her creative suggestions

The unexamined life is not worth living

Socrates

QUALITIES OF A PSYCHOTHERAPIST

Dear John, You asked me what I consider essential personal qualities in a future psychoanalyst. The answer is comparatively simple. If you want to be a real psychoanalyst you have to have a great love of the truth, scientific truth as well as personal truth, and you have to place this appreciation of truth higher than any discomfort at meeting unpleasant facts, whether they belong to the world outside or to your own inner person. Further, I think that a psychoanalyst should have... interests... beyond the limits of the medical field... in facts that belong to sociology, religion, literature, [and] history,... [otherwise] his outlook on... his patient will remain too narrow. This point contains... the necessary preparations beyond the requirements made on candidates of psychoanalysis in the institutes. You ought to be a great reader and become acquainted with the literature of many countries and cultures. In the great literary figures you will find people who know at least as much of human nature as the psychiatrists and psychologists try to do.

Does that answer your question?

ANNA FREUD

Contents

INTRODUCTION
By
Dr. Rizwan Ali

I am so glad that you decided to read this book. After you finish reading it, we the writers expect you to have a better understanding of the basic principles of psychodynamics and different schools of psychology influencing our current psychodynamic formulation. But first, let me tell you why we decided to write this book in the first place!

Psychotherapy is as much an art as it is a science. Learning this art is a tedious job which requires interest, patience and compassion. One also needs a skilled and trained teacher who knows the art of teaching psychotherapy. We need an inquisitive person with a keen interest in the intricate details of the psychological mysteries of the mind, and an empathic heart which can feel the pain and suffering of the individual before us.

Since 1991, when I decided to become a psychiatrist, I have never regretted a day or felt bored with my work. I have been teaching psychotherapy and psychodynamic formulation to senior residents in a psychiatry training program for the last eleven years. During one of my very introductory lectures I make it very clear to my students that this training and understanding of the human mind is what makes us unique as mental health care providers (psychiatrists, psychologists, nurses and social workers). A primary care physician can diagnose and prescribe medications for depression or anxiety, but to write a psychodynamic formulation and to select a patient for an appropriate treatment modality is a very special task that is learned in the advanced years of psychiatry and psychology training. This art of writing a psychodynamic formulation makes us stand out in the field of medicine.

It is also true that not everyone is naturally equipped to be a psychotherapist or a psychoanalyst. Interests and priorities vary greatly. But it is also very important to undertake the training and hone the skills which make us a true psychiatrist/psychologist. Later in our professional lives we can decide how much of that psychodynamic training we want to practice. Some of my colleagues practice biological psychiatry (psychopharmacology – prescribing medications for mental illnesses) and psychodynamic psychiatry at a 50:50 split, while some do it in an 80:20 ratio. This means that they practice biological/medical psychiatry which is focused on diagnosis of psychiatric illness and prescription of medications eighty percent of the time and while doing so, they provide some supportive and dynamic therapy as well. Whichever proportion suits your temperament and economics is fine, but there is no excuse for this important skill being overlooked. Some very busy and experienced psychiatrists love to practice only psychodynamic psychiatry and they leave medication management to their fellow psychiatrists or general practitioners. It is all about personal interest and making the right choices based on those personal interests. As Glen Gabbard noted in his book *Psychodynamic Psychiatry*, "the dynamic psychiatrist who neglects the neurobiological underpinnings of experience is as guilty of reductionism as the biologically oriented psychiatrist who neglects the life of the mind".

I have known Dr. Khalid Sohail for more than twenty years. We have discussed and shared interests in various topics including theater, music, poetry, literature and several other creative and social issues. The main connection that we share together is our passion for psychiatry and mainly psychodynamics and psychotherapy. Dr. Sohail has been practicing psychotherapy for decades and has written several books on the art and practice of psychotherapy. When he invited me to co-author this book on becoming a psychotherapist, I felt honored and humbled at the same time—honored because Dr. Sohail has published close to fifty books on different and varied subjects and this will be my first book, even though I have written chapters in a few books in the past; humbled because he is a well-known psychotherapist, poet, creative writer and an intellectual, across North America and beyond, and to link my name with his is indeed a humbling experience for me. I felt excited as well, because teaching psychotherapy is close to my heart and I feel very passionate writing or talking about it.

As the outstanding psychiatrist John C. Nemiah wrote, "It would be far easier if we could avoid the patient as we explore the realm of psychopathology; it would be far simpler if we could limit ourselves to examining the chemistry and physiology of his brain, and to treating mental events as objects alien to our immediate experience, or as mere variables in impersonal statistical formulae. Important as these approaches are for the understanding of human behavior, they cannot alone uncover or explain all the relevant facts. To see into the mind of another, we must repeatedly immerse ourselves in the flood of his associations and feelings; we must be ourselves the instrument that sounds him."

This book is divided into two sections. The first covers basic psychodynamic principles and the second addresses advanced psychodynamic concepts with a comprehensive discussion on psychodynamic formulation and the art of patient selection. The first section lays the ground for beginners and novice readers, giving a historical perspective on different schools of psychology and their impact on modern conceptualization and the understanding of the human mind. Dr. Sohail has done an excellent job of bringing his own personal stories into his journey of becoming a successful psychotherapist. He also talks about his "Green Zone Therapy" which is a unique and helpful concept in the field of psychotherapy. The advanced section is written by me for readers with some training. The chapters in the advanced section of this book are the essence of my eleven years of teaching the art of psychodynamic formulation to senior psychiatry residents. Once a reader goes through the basic section, I think it will be easier for the beginners as well to understand the advanced section. After reading this book, both Dr. Sohail and I expect psychiatry residents and psychology interns, after reading this book, to be able to write a comprehensive formulation based on a bio-psycho-social model with a detailed treatment plan for their patients. As we all know, in learning psychotherapy, face-to-face supervision and direct feedback from a teacher is of the utmost importance, so this book may be useful as a reference, but it cannot take the place of a teacher. Before, during and after the formal training of the mental health professionals, this book can be used as a reference throughout their lives.

We also tried to keep the language very simple and deliberately tried to stay away from complicated phrases and technical jargon so that it would be easy for the general public to read. We expect our patients and their families to be able to read this material as well. It is our desire that after reading this book, they would be knowledgeable about the process of psychotherapy and the different schools of psychology. This information will ultimately help them understand the terminology which therapists sometimes use, and also be able to self-analyze and ultimately become their own therapists.

This book may also help other allied professionals who are involved in the care of psychiatric patients, but do not practice psychotherapy. Nurses, social workers, occupational therapists, crisis workers and case managers may find this book very helpful in their understanding of the inner psychological conflicts of their patients and of the process by which trained clinicians devise treatment plans.

Both of us believe that by making psychiatric literature easier to comprehend, we will reach more people in the community, and that the increased understanding of mental illnesses will ultimately help us eradicate the stigma attached to them – a stigma, which can be *internal* when it prevents a person from seeking help, and *external* when society perceives mental illness as a defect or disability. I hope we succeeded in our efforts. Only you can tell us that after reading this book and giving us your precious and valuable feedback. Thank-you!

Dr. K. Sohail/Dr. Rizwan Ali

SECTION ONE: BASIC PRINCIPLES OF PSYCHOTHERAPY BY DR. KHALID SOHAIL

Chapter One

FROM MEDICINE TO PSYCHIATRY

HIPPOCRATES: THE FATHER OF MEDICINE

Nearly 2500 years ago, the son of a Greek physician became the father of secular medicine. Born on the Greek island of Kos in 460 BC, he is known throughout the world as Hippocrates. The history of medicine would be incomplete without the inclusion of his name and contributions.

Hippocrates was the first physician who separated medicine from religion. He was the first to focus on the importance of finding natural rather than supernatural causes of human sufferings. Hippocrates realized that when people became physically sick, some of them believed that they had sinned and that the gods were punishing them, while others thought that they were possessed by demons. Hippocrates questioned these religious beliefs about sin and guilt. He presented alternate secular theories and based on his clinical observations and experiences, proved that human ailments were related to faulty diet, lack of exercise and unhealthy lifestyle. He suggested to his patients that rather than praying and offering sacrifices to please the gods, they should try to eat a balanced diet, take regular exercise and adopt a healthy lifestyle to improve their quality of life. He thought walking was the best medicine.

Hippocrates offered a Humoral Theory to explain medical illnesses. He believed that there were four body fluids or humors: blood, yellow bile, black bile and phlegm, and an imbalance in those fluids caused sickness. To regain health, the balance in those fluids needed to be restored.

Hippocrates was a kind, caring and compassionate physician. He emphasized that physicians should take their profession very seriously. He suggested that they keep medical records so that if another physician had to look after their patients in their absence, they could obtain guidance from their clinical records.

Hippocrates also suggested a code of ethics that we know as the Hippocratic Oath. He emphasized that physicians, if they cannot help their patients, must be careful not to hurt them. He was reluctant to use remedies if he was not sure about their effectiveness. Rather than suggesting drugs and herbs, he chose to focus on rest, the use of clean water, and healthy food. He believed in the healing power of nature and physicians working with nature to heal their patients. Hippocrates was a great believer in the laws of nature.

Hippocrates paid a heavy price for challenging the local religious and medical practices—he was imprisoned for twenty years. During his time in prison, rather than becoming depressed or angry, he compiled the principles and practices of his secular medicine in a book, *The Complicated Body,* which became part of his collected works known as *Hippocratic Corpus.* The *Corpus* remained a textbook for physicians for centuries.

Hippocrates was trained by his father and grandfather who were physicians. He had two sons, Thessalus and Draco, and a son-in-law, Polybus, who became his students and practiced Hippocrates' art and science of secular medicine. Hippocrates had another dedicated student, Soranus, who wrote Hippocrates's biography and documented many of his life stories.

After his release from prison, Hippocrates traveled as far as Thessaly, Thrace and the Sea of Marmora, teaching medicine. He died in Larissa at the age of 100.

The tradition of Hippocrates was admired by philosophers like Plato, and his practices were adopted by famous physicians like Galen and Ibn Sina.

Hippocrates became an integral part of medical history because he was the first physician to establish the discipline of medicine on the basis of secular science, separated from religious dogma and superstitions. For that, he is known as the Father of Medicine, and still revered by physicians worldwide. His Hippocratic Oath remains a guide for all schools and colleges of physicians that regulate the secular ethics of physicians, ensuring that they do not harm their patients and maintain a high standard of medical practice.

HUMORAL THEORY

In the last chapter, I touched upon Hippocrates' concept of bodily humors, the basis of early medical theory and practice. His Humoral Theory is worth a closer examination, as it governed medical care for centuries. Many Greek and Roman physicians and philosophers accepted that human health was based on the balance of four humors of the body. According to this theory, human beings had four kinds of temperaments, depending upon which humor played a dominant role.

The four humors according to Humoral medicine are:

Black bile: *Melanie chole*

Yellow bile: *chole*

Phlegm: *phlegma*

Blood: *haima*

The Greeks believed that the four humors were also related to four elements of the universe:

Black bile with earth

Yellow bile with fire

Phlegm with water

Blood with air

The physician and philosopher Galen (AD 129 – 216), also known as Jalinoos, described how the four humors were also connected with the four temperaments of human beings:

Black bile: related to Melancholic Temperament. People with this temperament appear serious, introverted, even suspicious. They are prone to depressed mood and sad behavior.

Yellow bile: related to Choleric Temperament. People with such temperament are excitable, restless and impulsive. They are prone to angry and aggressive behavior.

Phlegm: related to Phlegmatic Temperament. People with such temperament are private, calm, tolerant and patient. They are prone to apathetic behavior.

Blood: related to Sanguine Temperament and connected with lively, talkative and pleasure seeking behavior. They are prone to being chronically late and forgetful.

Avicenna (980 – 1037 AD), a well-respected Iranian Muslim physician philosopher, in his famous book *The Canon of Medicine* that remained a textbook of medicine for many centuries in different parts of the world, extended the theory of temperaments to encompass emotional states, mental attitudes and psychological problems.

According to Humoral Theory, human beings were healthy when all four humors were in a balance. When that balance was disturbed, a person suffered and their symptoms depended upon which humor was in excess. Physicians helped their patients to regain their balance so that they could again lead a healthy and happy life.

GALEN: THE PHILOSOPHER PHYSICIAN
129 AD--216 AD

Galen, also known in the East as Jalinoos, was a Greek physician who made significant contributions to the tradition of medicine and surgery. He was inspired by the Humoral theory of Hippocrates. His reputation was such that that he became a personal physician to many emperors of his time.

Galen had a keen interest in human anatomy and physiology. Since dissection of human cadavers was illegal in Greece and Rome, Galen chose to dissect pigs and monkeys. Through these investigations, he developed his theories about the brain controlling the muscles and the larynx generating the voice. He was an excellent surgeon and used to say that wounds were the windows of the body.

Galen also believed in natural rather than supernatural causes of human illnesses and helped his patients benefit from the healing qualities of nature.

He was interested as well in human psychology and philosophy. He believed that the human intellect and soul had three parts: the rational soul resided in the brain; the spiritual soul resided in heart; and the appetitive soul resided in the liver.

In his lifetime he became so famous that Emperor Marcus Aurelius said, "Galen is first among doctors and unique among philosophers." Galen has inspired many physicians over the centuries including Ibn Sina. His books were translated into Arabic by the Syrian scholar Hunayn Ibn Ishaq in 830-870 AD and promoted by Zakaria Rhazes in 865–925 AD. Galen's theories about human anatomy and physiology were accepted for more than a thousand years until they were challenged by Andreas Vesalius in the 16th century, as he was able to dissect human cadavers.

Galen used to say that the best physician is also a philosopher.

IBN SINA AND THE *CANON OF MEDICINE*

When I was a medical student at Khyber Medical College, Peshawar Pakistan, I loved to read the college magazine *Sina* as it was named after the famous Persian physician, philosopher and scholar Ibn Sina, known in the Western world as Avicenna. In my final year I felt proud to be the editor of that prestigious magazine.

When I was in Iran, I worked in a children's hospital in Hamadan. From the window of my clinic I could see the tomb of Ibn Sina. Ibn Sina spent many years of his life in Hamadan creating his masterpieces in medicine and philosophy. It gave me great pleasure to walk on the streets that Ibn Sina had walked a thousand years ago.

Ibn Sina was born in 980 AD in Afsana, a village near Bukhara. His father Abdullah, a well-respected scholar, made sure that Ibn Sina received the best education available. As a teenager, Ibn Sina developed a strong interest in medicine and philosophy. He was troubled by Aristotle's *Metaphysics*; he read it many times and did not rest until he read the commentary by al Farabi.

As a young adult, Ibn Sina traveled to many cities, countries and cultures. He read and wrote extensively. Finally he settled in Hamadan where he died in 1037 AD. He summarized his philosophy thus: "I prefer a short life with width to a narrow one with length."

Ibn Sina had a wide range of interests from medicine to psychology, poetry to philosophy, logic to theology. He considered prophets "inspired philosophers" and human intellect "divine light". George Sarton, author of *The History of Science*, described Ibn Sina as "one of the greatest thinkers and medical scholars in history."

Ibn Sina wrote more than two hundred works, the two most famous of which are *The Book of Healing* and *Canon of Medicine*. He completed his five-volume masterpiece *Canon of Medicine* in 1025. In that book he synthesized and integrated Hippocratic, Aristotelian, Galenic, Chinese, Arab and Persian traditions. It was like an encyclopedia of medicine. The term *canon* had Latin and Ancient Greek origins that meant *measuring rod* and *standard*. It is one of the most respected books of medical history and remained a textbook in universities all over the word for nearly eight hundred years.

In the *Canon of Medicine* Ibn Sina stated that medicine was a science as well as an art. He wrote, "Medicine is the science by which we learn the various states of the body; in health, when not in health, the means by which health is likely to be lost, and, when lost, is likely to be restored. In other words, it is the art whereby health is concerned and the art by which it is restored after being lost." Ibn Sina made significant contributions to Humoral Theory and added a psychological dimension to physical medicine. In his book he wrote a special chapter on Melancholia, now known as depression.

Ibn Sina's *Canon of Medicine* has been translated into many languages.

RECENT ADVANCES IN PSYCHIATRY

There was a time in history when it was believed that people had mental problems because they had sinned or they were possessed by demons and spirits. Some religious clerics performed exorcism to cure mental patients. Hippocrates was the first physician who believed in natural rather than supernatural causes of physical illnesses and mental sufferings. Hippocrates once visited his philosopher friend Democritus who was dissecting animals and when Hippocrates asked him what he was looking for, Democritus stated that he was trying to discover the causes of madness and melancholy.

When we study the history of mental asylums we realize that some of the earliest hospitals for mental patients were built in 705 AD in Baghdad and in 800 AD in Cairo. They were called *bimaaristans* where patients were treated with respect and regard. Some of them even offered music therapy.

Galen and Ibn Sina were the first physicians who in their writings about mental disorders explained those conditions with their Humoral Theory. They believed that Melanchole was caused by increased levels of black bile in the body. In 1621 Robert Burton wrote the first book on mental illness titled *The Anatomy of Melancholy* in which he described a melancholic woman who got better when she fell in love. Burton also believed that becoming active helps people to recover from melancholy. His famous quotation is "no greater cause of melancholy than idleness, no better cure than business." After Burton, in 1758 William Battle wrote his *Treatise of Madness* discussing how people with mental disorders could be helped. He criticized Bethlem (Bedlam) Hospital for the mentally ill which provided only custodial care. Battle recommended good food, fresh air, regular exercise and supervised activities for patients. In those years, many of the inmates were chained as they were considered dangerous.

In the 18th century a movement known as Moral Treatment strove to liberate the mentally ill from neglectful and punitive conditions. French physician Philippe Pinel and British physician William Tuke are considered the founders of the movement. Pinel, as chief physician of Bicetre Hospital in France, freed patients from their chains in 1797, a major step towards humane treatment of the mentally ill in Europe.

For many years, hospitals for those suffering from mental illness were called madhouses and lunatic asylums. Vienna's "madhouse" also known as the "fools' tower" was built in 1784.

In the 19th century the discipline of Phrenology developed. Johann Spurzheim (1776—1832) delivered lectures in hospitals and universities regarding his craniological concepts and correlated mental disorders with diseases of the brain. He discussed mental disorders in neurological rather than philosophical and religious terms, which was a breakthrough in psychiatry.

In England in 1845, the Lunacy Act was passed which ensured humane treatment for the mentally ill rather than just custodial care. Lord Shaftesbury and other enlightened political activists were involved in that movement. In the 19th century the number of mental hospitals increased from hundreds to thousands.

The term *psychiatry* was coined by Johann Christian Reil in 1808, meaning the discipline of healing the mind.

In the 20th century there have been numerous breakthroughs in the tradition of psychiatry. Emil Kraeplin pursued the idea of classification of mental disorders, an idea presented by Karl Kahlbaum. Such classification focused on etiology as well as symptomatology, and considered the biological, psychological and social causes of mental disorders.

While the discoveries of Sigmund Freud and other psychoanalysts developed the traditions of psychotherapy and psychoanalysis, there grew in parallel the disciplines of biological psychiatry and psychopharmacology. Otto Loewi was the first to discover a neurotransmitter, acetylcholine, in the brain, followed by discoveries of other neurotransmitters like dopamine, nor-adrenaline and serotonin. It was believed that in mental illnesses there are biochemical disorders of the brain that can be helped by psychotropic drugs including major and minor tranquilizers, anti-anxiolytics and anti-depressants.

The first anti-psychotic, Chlorpromazine, was discovered in 1952 and used to treat schizophrenia; and the first mood stabilizer, Lithium Carbonate, was made available in 1948 to treat bipolar disorder. After those medications, other anti-psychotics, anti-anxiety, anti-depressants and mood stabilizers came into use.

In the 20th century, a number of psychiatric research studies were done to discover the genetic patterns of mental illnesses including schizophrenia and manic depressive illness.

Because of increased interest in humane and respectful treatment of those with mental illness, many individuals were discharged from psychiatric hospitals to live in supportive housing and obtain their treatment in the community with a combination of medications, education and psychotherapy. Those treatment modalities followed the bio-psycho-social model of mental health.

HAVE THE TIMES CHANGED?

There was a time when people with mental illness used to wander around half naked in the streets and people threw rocks at them.

There was a time when communities used to put mentally ill people in madhouses and bind them with chains.

There was a time when doctors who treated mentally ill people were called alienists.

There was a time when people believed that human beings became mentally ill because of the full moon. Because of that association with the moon, they were called lunatics and the places they were kept were called lunatic asylums.

There was a time that people believed that mentally ill people were possessed by ghosts, demons and witches.

There was a time that people believed that mental illness was caused by sins and could be cured by exorcism.

Then people's thinking changed and they began to believe in natural rather than supernatural causes of mental illness. They came to believe that mental illness was related to abnormalities of the body and the brain rather than sins and spirits.

Alienists became psychiatrists, lunatic asylums became psychiatric hospitals, and psychiatry became an extension of neurology and medicine.

Mental illness became known as psychosis and classified as schizophrenia and manic depressive illness; and emotional problems became known as neurosis and personality problems.

Psychiatrists, doctors and researchers discovered that mental illnesses and emotional problems could be treated with medications, education and psychotherapy.

In many parts of the world doctors and nurses, psychologists and social workers began to work together as mental health professionals to care for mentally ill people and their families.

In the hospitals and clinics of many communities, mental health professionals adopted the bio-psycho-social model which meant that mental illnesses and emotional problems are caused by a combination of biological factors including genetic and biochemical factors; psychological factors including childhood and personality factors; and social factors including family and cultural factors.

Mental health professionals realized that to care for people with mental illnesses and emotional problems, we need to treat them with a combination of psychotropic medications including anti-psychotics, antidepressants and anti-anxiety medications, and psychotherapies including individual, marital, family and group therapy, depending upon the needs of the patients and their families.

In the 21st century, while times have changed in many communities, countries and cultures, there are other communities, countries and cultures where mentally ill people still wander around half-naked in the streets and people throw rocks at them or they are locked up in madhouses and bound with chains or they are taken to spiritual healers for exorcism. In such communities and cultures, the mentally ill and the people who care for them remain stuck in the dark ages, awaiting the liberating light of scientific knowledge and humane treatment.

Chapter Two

DIFFERENT SCHOOLS OF HUMAN PSYCHOLOGY

ENCOUNTERS WITH THE HUMAN PSYCHE

INTRODUCTION

Over the centuries, the human psyche has remained a mystery for professionals as well as lay people. In the last century a number of psychologists, psychotherapists, scholars and philosophers have tried to solve that mystery and have developed different schools of human psychology. The ideas, concepts and theories presented by these schools have helped us understand

… complexities of the mind

…characteristics of the human personality

and

…dynamics of emotional problems.

Based on these discoveries, mental health professionals are able to help patients and their families decrease human suffering and increase human happiness. Their insights also guide people to lead healthy, happy and peaceful lives. Their experiences inspire people to focus on their personal growth and discover their full potential.

These philosophers have helped millions of people all over the world to lead healthy and happy lives individually and collectively. In this essay I will focus on different schools of human psychology that developed in the 20th century.

FIRST SCHOOL:
SIGMUND FREUD AND THE PSYCHOANALYTICAL
SCHOOL

Sigmund Freud, the father of psychoanalysis, was originally a physician and a neurologist. He developed a keen interest in the unconscious mind when his father died in 1896. Freud was in his late thirties at that time. For the next three years he analyzed his own dreams and in 1900 published his masterpiece *Interpretation of Dreams* which has been read by his disciples as the Bible of psychoanalysis.

Freud started developing his theories when his older colleague Joseph Breuer referred to him a young patient known in the psychoanalytic literature as Anna O, who suffered from hysteria, a common condition in women at that time in Vienna and Europe. While Breuer was treating her hysterical symptoms, Anna O fell in love with him and declared that she was pregnant. Breuer, who was a married man and a respectable doctor in his community, became alarmed and left town to protect his social image.

When Freud started treating Anna O, he discovered that she was not pregnant. It was one the symptoms of her clinical condition. As Freud analyzed the case he concluded that her hysteria was the result of unresolved sexual conflicts of the patient's childhood. Later on Freud and Breuer jointly wrote a paper on Hysteria sharing their clinical observations and experiences.

As Freud developed his treatment method he called it psychoanalysis. One of the salient features of this method was the recognition that patient transfers her feelings from her past to the therapist, which he called *transference;* and psychotherapy helps the patient to resolve those feelings so that she can live in reality and not project the past into the present. As the patient resolves her transference, she can let go of the symptoms and become cured.

Freud investigated a series of patients day after day, week after week, month after month, year after year, as they lay on the couch doing free association while he sat in chair behind the patient taking notes and smoking his cigar. Freud's clinic in Vienna became the labor room that gave birth to the philosophy and practice of psychoanalysis. In that clinic he developed the concept of *repression,* in which the patient pushes the painful experiences down into the unconscious mind, as well as other defense mechanisms like denial, projection, rationalization and magical thinking that give rise to psychological symptoms of anxiety, depression, panic disorder and other neurotic disorders.

With the help of free association and psychoanalysis, Freud helped his patients bring unconscious unresolved conflicts to the conscious mind and then deal with them realistically to heal and free themselves of symptoms.

Alongside unhealthy defense mechanisms, Freud also developed the concept of healthy coping mechanisms like humor, creativity and sublimation which mature people use to cope with their emotional conflicts and social dilemmas. By the coping mechanism of sublimation, people find a socially acceptable way to express their immature instinctive needs. For example, a man with strong aggressive instincts might become a boxer; or a woman who wants to expose herself might become an actress; and people who want to drive fast and break traffic rules might become ambulance drivers. Sublimation helps them acquire a socially acceptable lifestyle.

Freud developed a detailed theory of personality using the concepts of Id, Ego and Superego, Conscious, Preconscious and Unconscious mind and oral, anal, phallic and genital stages of development. If any developmental stage is disturbed, then the person has symptoms of that stage in their adult life. For example, people with addictions have unresolved issues of the oral stage and need to excessively smoke cigarettes, eat food or drink alcohol to satisfy their unresolved emotional needs. Freud linked different personalities with instincts and developmental stages of childhood. He also introduced the concept of Oedipus Complex in which a boy loves his mother and hates his father as he does not want to share his mother with his father. For his psycho-sexual maturity, he has to resolve his Oedipus Complex to let go of his mother to his father and find another woman to love. Freud borrowed the concept from Greek mythology. If the man does not resolve his Oedipus complex successfully, then he remains attached to his mother and cannot love another woman wholeheartedly and experiences problems in his marriage and love life. In girls, it is called the Electra Complex, the dynamics and resolution of which are more complex than in boys.

Although Freud was brought up in a Jewish family he was very critical of the institution of religion. His books *Moses and Monotheism* and *Future of an Illusion* highlight his philosophy in which he compares neurosis with religion. He believed that religion was a cultural neurosis and neurosis was a personalized religion. His prediction was that as the borders of science would expand, the borders of religion would shrink.

Freud was a compassionate therapist but in his personal life he was quite authoritarian. When he established the Psychoanalytical Institute, he welcomed his colleagues and friends; but he had a difficult time dealing with people who challenged his authority, personality and philosophy. That cost him the friendships of many of his colleagues.

Freud died in 1939 by taking an overdose of opium as he suffered from the cancer of jaw for which numerous operations had failed to control his pain. Even that cancer and pain did not stop him from smoking his cigars till the last days of his life.

After Freud's death a number of philosophers, psychologists and psychotherapists promoted and developed his theories. His daughter Anna Freud, a child analyst, discovered more defense mechanisms while doing therapy with children. Eric Fromm combined theories of Sigmund Freud with those of Karl Marx and wrote books like *Escape from Freedom, Beyond the Chains of Illusion, My Encounter with Marx and Freud* and *The Sane Society* and offered psychoanalytic interpretations of cultural behaviors that people adopt in both socialistic and capitalistic societies. He built bridges between human psychology and sociology. Peter Sifneos, Habib Davanloo and many other modern psychotherapists developed the practice of Short Term Dynamic Psychotherapy using the psychodynamic principles of Freud.

While there were many admirers and disciples, Freud also had a number of critics. Some anthropologists stated that Freud's concept of Oedipus Complex was a reflection of his observations of European nuclear families and did not apply to the extended family and tribal systems still prevalent in many parts of Asia, the Middle East and Africa. Many experimental psychologists and behaviorists like Hans Eysenck, Albert Ellis and Burrhus Frederic Skinner criticized Freud for focusing on abstract unconscious motives rather than concrete observable behaviors. Karl Popper, the scientific philosopher, believed that a theory could become part of science only if it could be proved wrong. Since Freud's theories of the Oedipus Complex and the unconscious mind cannot be disproved, they might be useful and therapeutic but still remain part of psychology and philosophy, rather than science.

Although Freud shared his theories with physicians and scientists, he surprisingly received a Goethe Award for literature, as in his lifetime he was appreciated by artists and writers far more than physicians and scientists. He influenced not only practices of mental health, but also education, fine arts and culture.

SECOND SCHOOL:
CARL JUNG
AND THE
SCHOOL OF ANALYTICAL PSYCHOLOGY

Carl Jung was a Swiss psychiatrist who made valuable contributions to our understanding of human psychology. He became famous for his ideas about the personality types of Introversion and Extraversion, and his concept of Collective Unconscious.

While Jung was practicing in Zurich, he had a special interest in psychiatric patients and developed a Word Association Experiment to study their thought patterns. When he wrote his paper, he sent it to Sigmund Freud who became curious and expressed a desire to meet Jung. Jung was 30 and Freud was 50 at that time. In 1907 they met for the first time and talked for nearly 12 hours non-stop. Freud was so impressed that he called Jung his "son". They started working together and in 1911 they founded the International Psychoanalytical Association and Jung became its first president. It did not take long for Jung to discover that Freud could not tolerate other people disagreeing with him. While Freud had a special interest in human sexuality, Jung had a keen interest in human spirituality. They challenged each other and finally stopped talking; their friendship ended in 1913. Jung was so upset by that breakup that he had a breakdown. When he recovered, he started his own school called Analytical Psychology. Jung wrote a number of books to share his ideas and became quite popular.

Some of the concepts presented by Jung are as follows:

1. Collective Unconscious. Jung believed that human beings not only have a personal unconscious but they are also connected with a collective unconscious. Such unconscious can be seen in art and music, poetry and folktales of any culture and also in people's dreams.

2. Dreams. Jung believed that our dreams not only reflect our past but also communicate things about our future.

3. Archetypes. The Collective Unconscious is connected to archetypes that are shared by all of humanity. They are like our psychic DNAs.

4. Psychological Problems. Jung believed that mental health is reflected in a balanced relationship between conscious and unconscious minds. When that balance is disturbed, people suffer from neurosis and

personality disorder, and if the conscious mind is flooded by the unconscious material, people have a psychotic breakdown.

5. Self-realization. As human beings grow and mature they become more self-realized. Jung believed that a cooperative relationship between the collective unconscious and self-realization helps people in their emotional growth and maturity so that they become more spiritual.

6. Shadow. When unpleasant and painful experiences and memories are repressed, they become part of the Shadow Self. Many people use denial and projection to deal with their shadow part.

7. Anima / Animus. Jung believed that men had an unconscious feminine part that he called anima, and women had an unconscious male part that he called animus. Healthy people try to integrate their two sides. Such integration is seen in older people.

8. Wise Men and Women. Jung believed that those men and women who can deal with their dark side and integrate different sides of their personality become wise men and women.

Before Jung died in his 80s he wrote his autobiography entitled *Memories, Dreams,*

Reflections in which he shared the highlights of his psychological, professional and spiritual journey.

Over the decades the number of mental health professionals and lay people who are inspired by Jung's writings has increased.

THIRD SCHOOL
ALFRED ADLER
AND
THE SCHOOL OF INDIVIDUAL PSYCHOLOGY
Alfred Adler (1870-1937) was an Austrian doctor who became a psychotherapist and founder of the school of Individual Psychology.

Adler was a contemporary of Sigmund Freud. He met Freud in 1902 and was a member of the Psychoanalytical Society for a few years. He became President of the Vienna Psychoanalytical Society in 1910. In the beginning Freud admired Adler's ideas, but when he started challenging Freud's theories, he was asked to leave his group. After saying goodbye to the psychoanalytical school in 1911, Adler started his own school of human psychology in 1912 and called it Individual Psychology.

Alder believed that every human being is an indivisible whole that cannot be divided into parts. That is why we call human beings individuals.

Adler also believed that for healthy living, human beings need to be connected with their social circle in a meaningful way. Adler was inspired by socialist philosophy. He believed that the external social life of human beings is as important as their internal emotional life. He introduced a socially-oriented approach to psychology.

Adler was the first one who changed the therapy session from a couch and a chair to two chairs. Using a chair for the patient and another chair for the therapist brought both human beings together at a symbolically equal level.

Adler also broke away from the elitist attitude of psychoanalysts who wrote in very academic and difficult language; he wrote in simple language that lay people could understand. He believed in public education about mental health.

Alder introduced the concept of *inferiority complex* to human psychology. He was the first one who emphasized the significance of self-esteem in the human personality. He showed that people with low self-esteem suffered emotionally. He promoted the concept of *will to power* that inspires people to use their creative power to change their lives for the better.

Adler, alongside Freud and Jung, is considered one of the three pioneers of in-depth psychology.

Adler also inspired Victor Frankl. Frankl, in his book *Man's Search for Meaning* considers his logo-therapy school of therapy the *Third Viennese School of Psychotherapy*, after the Freudian Psychoanalytical School and the Adlerian School of Individual Psychology. Frankl highlighted that Freud believed in the *pleasure principle,* Adler believed in *will to power,* while Frankl himself believed in *will to meaning.*

Adler died in 1937 in Aberdeen, Scotland, of a heart attack during a lecture tour. He was cremated but his ashes went missing for a long time until they were found in 2007.

Adler influenced many psychologists including Rollo May, Victor Frankl, Abraham Maslow and Albert Ellis. Adler was a social idealist and a humanist. He was one of the pioneers of the Humanist School in human psychology and psychotherapy.

FOURTH SCHOOL:
HARRY STACK SULLIVAN AND THE
INTERPERSONAL SCHOOL

Harry Stack Sullivan was the founder of the Interpersonal School of therapy. While Freud believed that anxiety was an intra-psychic phenomenon, Sullivan believed that it was an interpersonal experience. Sullivan believed that when people are involved in conflicted relationships, they experience anxiety.

Sullivan also believed that low self-esteem played a major role in the genesis of emotional suffering. Sullivan introduced the concepts of Good Me, Bad Me and Not Me. He believed that when children receive positive sentiments from their parents and grandparents, aunts and uncles, teachers and principals who tell them

> You are smart
>
> You are beautiful
>
> You are charming

they gradually internalize those ideas and start believing

> I am smart
>
> I am beautiful
>
> I am charming

and develop Good Me.

On the other hand when children hear

>You are stupid
>
>You are ugly
>
>You are lazy

they gradually internalize those ideas and start believing

>I am stupid
>
>I am ugly
>
>I am lazy

and develop Bad Me.

Sullivan believed that in emotionally healthy people, Good Me is bigger than Bad Me, while in people with emotional problems, Bad Me is larger than Good Me.

Sullivan had a unique theory of psychosis. He believed that when the Bad Me becomes so big that it becomes unbearable and intolerable for people, then a part of Bad Me breaks down and turns into Not Me. That is when a person has a psychotic breakdown and starts hallucinating. Sullivan believed that it is less painful to hear voices of a devil or a ghost telling you "You are stupid" than saying to yourself "I am stupid".

Sullivan believed that helping psychiatric patients improve their self- esteem was crucial in their recovery and rehabilitation. He treated his patients with great respect. He had rented a house in New York where he admitted and treated his patients and hired ex-patients as his assistants.

While Freud believed in the pleasure principle and thought that human beings wanted to satisfy their libidinal desires, Sullivan believed that security was as important as satisfaction. He believed that when human beings do not feel secure within themselves and in their significant relationships they experience anxiety. He suggested that therapists should provide their patients with a secure relationship so that they can heal and develop positive self-esteem.

Sullivan's school of psychiatry became known as the Interpersonal School while in England Ronald Fairbairn's school with similar ideas became known as the Object Relations School. Fairbairn disagreed with Freud. Freud believed that the human psyche was pleasure-seeking while Fairbairn believed it was object-seeking. He believed that having a relationship was more important to people than having pleasure. That theory explains why so many people with poor self-esteem stay in unhealthy and abusive relationships, because for them having a bad relationship is better than having no relationship.

While Sullivan developed the idea of Good Me and Bad Me, Ronald Fairbairn and Melanie Klein developed the idea of Good Object and Bad Object that became part of the Object Relations Theory. Klein's and Fairbairn's ideas were further developed by another psychoanalyst named Otto Kernberg who made significant contributions towards understanding the dynamics of

Borderline and Narcissistic Personality Disorders.

Followers of the Object Relations Theory believe that a child goes through a number of developmental stages.

1st stage…When the child is born and fed by the mother, the child emotionally cannot separate himself from the mother, and cannot separate the self from the object.

2nd stage…The child keeps the good self-object representation separate from the bad self-object representation as the child cannot integrate the good with the bad.

3rd stage…The child separates good self from good object and bad self from bad object. The good and bad are kept apart by the defense of splitting.

4th stage…The good and bad self and good and bad object are integrated in the child.

5th stage…In this stage the id, ego and super-ego are consolidated and a mature personality is developed.

People who cannot separate self from others suffer from schizophrenia.

People who cannot integrate good me and bad me and good object from bad object suffer from Borderline Personality Disorder as they use the defense mechanism of splitting—splitting between good object and bad object. Therapy helps people with Borderline Personality Disorder integrate good and bad objects and experience the therapist and themselves as a whole.

The Interpersonal School and the Object Relations School highlighted the significance of the child's relationship with the mother and other nurturing figures. Their theories were confirmed by the studies conducted by psychologists like John Bowlby who developed the Attachment Theory and showed how people's emotional and romantic relationships as adults depend on their childhood relationships with their parents and other caring adults.

FIFTH SCHOOL:
MURRAY BOWEN AND THE SYSTEMS SCHOOL

While Sigmund Freud taught us the secrets of individual psychology and Harry Stack Sullivan guided us in understanding the mysteries of relationships, Murray Bowen shed light on the dynamics of family systems. I was so impressed by his philosophy that I flew to Virginia to listen to his lecture.

Of all the ideas that he presented in his family systems philosophy, I will share three important concepts.

1. Triangulation

Bowen believed that the primary unit of human relationships is a triangle. When two people involved in a relationship experience tension, one of them connects with the third party to relieve tension and the third person gets triangulated.

Bowen believed that in many dysfunctional families a child gets triangulated because the parents are unable to resolve their conflict respectfully and peacefully. Their marital tension is absorbed by the child and expressed in various symptoms. To prove his point Bowen treated some children suffering from bed wetting and truancy and other emotional problems without seeing the child. He treated the parents and as the parents resolved their conflicts, the child got better.

According to the theory of triangles, one spouse can initiate an affair to deal with marital conflict. According to this theory there are many marriages that survive because of an extra-marital affair. In many cases when the affair ends, after a short time the marriage ends too.

2. Emotional Cut-Off

Bowen believed that every person and every family system has an emotional cut-off point. Once the tension reaches that level a person starts to shut down emotionally. It can express itself by withdrawing or completely severing the ties with the family. When a member of the family has a breakdown and is removed from the family system, another person becomes vulnerable to have a breakdown. Bowen believed that mental health professionals need to help the whole family to resolve their emotional conflicts rather than treating only the identified patient. Bowen was critical of individual-focused treatment models.

When Bowen was doing his research on family systems, he used to admit the whole family for a few weeks in a cottage to assess the family dynamics. In that family the grandmother and the cat were as important as parents and children. He admitted all living beings that resided under one roof.

3. Emotional Differentiation

Bowen believed that each person can be seen on a spectrum of emotional differentiation, from 1 to 100. The ideal is 100 but it is not realistic. Those people who are more emotionally differentiated have a solid self, as a part of their personality. People with a solid self are emotionally mature and make wise choices about life. They have a set of values and principles that is based on their own life experiences and reflections. They are not easily influenced by other people or fleeting fashions. They do not over-react to circumstances and are not easily triangulated.

On the other hand people who are less emotionally differentiated have no solid self. Less differentiated people are emotionally labile and lead an unstable life. Small stresses can create major crises. Therapy helps such people to develop a solid self so that they can deal with emotional and social crises in a mature way and act wisely.

Bowen believed that intelligence is not related to emotional differentiation. Highly intelligent people can be least emotionally differentiated and may not have a solid core in their personality. People with a high I.Q. can be emotionally immature.

Before Murray Bowen died, he was trying to extend his concepts about family systems to social and cultural systems. He believed that like people and families, communities and cultures can be less or more mature and less and or more differentiated. Mature communities and cultures inspire their members to become more emotionally independent. But before Bowen could fully articulate his theory, he left this world.

SIXTH SCHOOL:
ALBERT ELLIS
AND
THE COGNITIVE BEHAVIOUR SCHOOL
Albert Ellis (1913-2007) was an American psychologist who pioneered the school of Cognitive Behavior Therapy. He received his PhD degree from Columbia University in 1947. In the beginning he was inspired by Sigmund Freud and psychoanalysis but later on he was influenced by Alfred Adler, Erich Fromm and Harry Stack Sullivan. Reading Alfred Korzybski's book *Science and Sanity* made a big impact on him and in the 1950s he discovered his own form of therapy. In the beginning he used to call himself a Rational Therapist. He believed that through rational thinking and cognitive reconstruction people could understand and change their self-destructive thought patterns to overcome their emotional problems. In the beginning other psychologists opposed his theories but over a period of time his philosophy became popular and more and more people started following his mode of therapy.

Albert Ellis was an atheist and a humanist and many religious people opposed him because of his personal philosophy of life. Ellis repeatedly stated that his Cognitive Behavior Therapy approach is independent of his personal views. To clarify his personal views he wrote a book titled *The Road to Tolerance*; and to elaborate his professional views and show how his Cognitive Behavior Approach can help religious people, he wrote *Counseling and Psychotherapy with Religious Persons: A Rational Behavior Therapy Approach.* In the 1990s he renamed his therapy *Rational Emotive Behavior Therapy* to highlight that in his approach to psychology cognition, emotion and behavior are interconnected.

On his 90th birthday he received messages from many leading professional and political figures including Bill Clinton and the Dalai Lama. In his eulogy of Albert Ellis in 2007, APA past president Frank Farley stated, "...psychology has had only of a handful of legendary figures who not only command attention across much of the discipline but also receive recognition from the public for their work. Albert Ellis was such a figure, known inside and outside of psychology for his outstanding originality, his provocative ideas, and his provocative personality."

Albert Ellis was respected by many psychologists who promoted and popularized his theories.

Ellis believed in the theory of ABC

A…any activating event

B…belief system

C…consequences

Ellis believed that different people are affected differently by the same event because they give different meanings to that event based on their philosophy, personality and ideology. He thought that people suffer emotionally because they have irrational beliefs.

In therapy he introduced

D…disproving the irrational beliefs

E…effecting change.

The more people have rational understanding and realistic interpretations of events, the less they suffer emotionally. They learn to accept the realities of life and find ways to lead a happy and healthy life.

SEVENTH SCHOOL:
ERICH FROMM AND THE CULTURAL SCHOOL

Erich Fromm was one of those psychologists who helped us see that the human personality is affected not only by the family but also by culture. Erich Fromm built a bridge between psychology and sociology as he was one of those few people who studied Karl Marx with the same enthusiasm as he studied Sigmund Freud.

Eric Fromm wrote a large number of books and articles. Some of his books that became popular are *Escape From Freedom, Man For Himself, The Art of Loving* and *The Anatomy of Human Destructiveness.*

Fromm highlighted that human beings were born free, but not very many people can embrace freedom. There are many who escape freedom. Fromm shared his ideas that some people escape from freedom by conforming to the majority, while others give control of their lives to other people. Some become destructive and destroy others before they are destroyed by others.

Fromm tried to broaden the theories of Freud by adding new ideas to them. While Freud focused on the basic sexual and emotional needs, Fromm discussed higher needs of humans that include the need

…to belong to relationships and groups,

…of rootedness,

and

..to have a philosophy of life.

In his book *The Anatomy of Human Destructiveness,* Fromm shared that animals have benign aggression. They attack and kill other animals only when they are hungry, but humans exhibit malignant aggression. They attach new meanings to aggression and find different social, cultural and religious reasons to kill. In some ways humans act worse than animals.

Fromm studied religious scriptures and offered secular interpretations. He believed that humans no longer need autocratic and religious morals, humans can now create secular ethics based on human intelligence, reason and conscience. Fromm made significant contributions to humanist philosophy and was given the Humanist of the Year award by the American Humanist Association in 1966.

Fromm shared his political views in his book *The Sane Society,* in which he is critical of American capitalism as well as Russian communism. He was a member of the socialist democratic movement. He did not like those religious and political organizations that stunt human growth as he was a great supporter of human freedom.

EIGHTH SCHOOL:
ERIK ERIKSON AND THE LIFE SPAN SCHOOL

While many psychoanalysts focused on early childhood development of the human personality, Erik Erikson broadened his study to the whole life span. He believed that human beings face a new challenge at each stage of life. For healthy development of personality, human beings have to deal with each challenge in a constructive and graceful way. Those who deal with the challenge successfully move on to the next stage and those who cannot, suffer.

Erikson presented a unique theory of human personality. He divided the entire life span of human beings into eight stages and identified the challenge of each stage.

1. Basic Trust vs Basic Mistrust. This stage covers the first year of life. Those children who receive nurturing and caring from the mother and other loving adults develop a basic trust in maternal figures and also learn to trust later on. On the other hand those children who do not get that love, care and nurturing develop mistrust in their mothers and have difficulties trusting other people as adults.

2. Autonomy vs Shame. This stage is from age 1 to age 3. In this stage, the child learns to learn some autonomy from the mother and learns to be toilet trained. Those children who are successful develop a sense of autonomy and independence, while those who are not successful develop a sense of shame

3. Initiative vs Guilt. This stage covers from age 3 to age 6. In this stage the child learns to take initiative and do things independent of the parents. Children learn to tie their shoe laces, get dressed and play independently. Those children who are successful develop a sense of motivation to do their projects independently in life, while those who are not successful feel guilty doing things on their own.

4. Competence vs Inferiority. This stage covers from age 6 to age 11. In this stage the child learns to feel competent and develops self-esteem and self-worth. Teachers play an important role in this stage. Those children who are successful feel confident and competent, while those who are not successful develop poor self-esteem and a sense of inferiority.

5. Identity vs Role Confusion. This is the adolescent stage that covers from age 12 to 18. Teenagers struggle with the question: Who am I? Parents who are secure let

children develop their own identity while those who are insecure and demand conformity make it difficult for their children to be independent. Such teenagers develop role confusion and feel lost and confused.

6. Intimacy vs Isolation. This is the early stage of adult life between age 18 and 35 in which human beings learn to have intimate relationships. Those who are successful develop healthy friendships and loving relationships. Those who are not successful feel isolated, alone and lonely.

7. Generativity vs Stagnation. This is the late stage of adult life between 35 and 64. In this stage human beings try to maintain a productive lifestyle. Those who are successful have stable and successful family, work and social lives. Those who are unsuccessful feel stagnant and non-productive. They start realizing that they have not used their talents constructively.

8. Ego Integrity vs Despair. This is the last stage of life from 64 to death. Human beings review their life in this stage. Those who are successful develop ego integrity and accept the positive and negative, the dilemmas and dreams, the struggles and successes of life gracefully. Those who are not successful develop a sense of failure and despair. They feel unhappy and

realize they have wasted their lives. Those who are successful can accept death with a sense of accomplishment while those who are unsuccessful have difficulties saying good bye to life.

Erik Erikson made valuable contributions to theories of human personality. He is the psychologist who introduced to the world the concept of Identity Crisis. He took our understanding of the development of the human personality to new heights and depths. He made us aware that personal growth is a dynamic process and extends from cradle to grave, from birth to death.

NINTH SCHOOL:
JEAN PAUL SARTRE AND THE
EXISTENTIALIST SCHOOL

In the 20th century, one of the schools of human psychology that became popular was the existentialist school. Philosophers of the existentialist school highlighted that human beings have a free will. They experience choices when they face life challenges. They can succumb to those challenges and experience ontological insecurity and existential despair or they can make wise choices and create a meaningful life for themselves and their dear ones. Let me focus on three existentialist philosophers.

The first one is Ludwig Binswanger. Binswanger (1881-1966) suggested that to understand human existence we can divide the experience into three dimensions.

1. The first dimension is human beings experiencing their inner world called *Eigenwelt*
2. The second dimension is human beings experiencing other human beings called *Mitwelt*

3. The third dimension is human beings experiencing the environment and the universe around them called *Unwelt*.

Binswanger had an opportunity to work with and learn from great psychologists and psychiatrists like Carl Jung, Eugen Bleuler and Sigmund Freud. He offered Freud refuge in 1938 in Switzerland.

Binswanger's contributions to human psychology, psychiatry and psychotherapy are significant as they emphasize subjective experiences of patients. Rather than judging their behaviors and interpreting their unconscious motives, Binswanger suggests that we ask our patients what meaning they give to their encounters with life. The Existential School of human psychology was a significant departure from the psycho-analytical school. Binswanger encouraged his patients to take control of their lives, feel empowered and make healthy choices.

The second philosopher is Karl Jaspers (1883- 1969). When I was studying at Memorial University Newfoundland, one of my professors Dr. John Hoenig introduced me to Jaspers as he had translated his 1000-page German masterpiece *General Psychopathology* into English.

Jaspers helped psychiatrists and psychologists understand the concepts of phenomenology. He discussed how the symptoms of psychiatric patients can be divided into two groups: problems of the form and the problems of the content. For example, a patient who cannot focus on his conversation and jumps from one topic to another has a formal thought disorder. On the other hand, a delusional person who believes that someone is poisoning him has a content thought disorder. Jaspers was a great supporter of human freedom.

The third philosopher is Jean Paul Sartre (1905 – 1980). Sartre made valuable contributions to the Existentialist School. He was a writer and a philosopher. He refused to accept the Nobel Prize for Literature in 1964 stating, "a writer should not allow himself to be turned into an institution." Sartre's statement that human beings are 'condemned to be free" highlights his philosophy that we have no choice but to have a choice. Not making a choice is also making a choice. Sartre challenged many religious traditions and deterministic ideologies and asserted human freedom. He focused on the philosophy that *existence precedes essence.* Human beings do not have a meaning in life other than what they give it themselves. He encouraged human beings to take responsibility for their lives and make them meaningful. His book *Being and Nothingness* and his collection of plays *No Exit* capture the essence of his philosophy.

Sartre was also quite vocal about his political views. He criticized the French government about its role in Algeria. When he was arrested for his civil disobedience activities, President Charles de Gaulle set him free, stating, "You don't arrest Voltaire."

Sartre's contributions to existentialist philosophy have also influenced the disciplines of human psychology and psychotherapy. Sartre challenged Sigmund Freud and psychoanalysis and suggested that we need to focus on our present *here and now* rather than being preoccupied with the past like the psychoanalysts. Exploring our freedom in the present can set us free to have a better and happier future.

Sartre's life-long love affair with a leading feminist Simone de Beauvoir was a source of inspiration for both. Sartre contributed to Simone's feminism and Simone contributed to Sartre's existentialism. Their fifty years of loving relationship ended when Sartre died in 1980. Since neither of them believed in life after death, Simone stated on Sartre's death, "Your death separated us and my death will not bring us together."

Existentialist philosophers broadened the existential horizons of human psychology and added new dimensions to our understanding of the human personality.

TENTH SCHOOL:
ABRAHAM MASLOW AND THE
HUMANIST SCHOOL

While many schools of human psychology focused on the sick part of the human personality, the humanist school focused on the healthy part and found ways to inspire people to express their full potential and lead a meaningful life. Of all the humanist philosophers and psychologists, let me focus on four of them.

The first humanist psychologist is Rollo May. His book *The Meaning of Anxiety* is an amazing book. It is based on May's PhD thesis. In that book he reviews many philosophical and psychological theories and suggests how people can understand and deal with their anxiety and face the dilemma of to be or not to be.

Roll May was impressed by theologian Paul Tillich and was so inspired by his book *The Courage to Be* that he named his own book *The Courage to Create*. May believed that human beings go through four stages of development.

1. Innocence Stage. In this stage child is not self conscious and just follows his drives.

2. Rebellion Stage. In this stage a teenager wants to rebel to gain his freedom but has not learnt to take responsibility for his rebellion and freedom.

3. Ordinary Stage. In this stage a person learns to take responsibility but finds it too stressful, so he conforms to the social and cultural traditions to make his life easier.

4. Creative Stage. In this stage a person learns to be authentic and is ready to pay the price to be non-traditional and creative.

May also wrote a book titled *Love and Will* that captures some of his humanist ideas and ideals.

The second humanist psychologist is Carl Rogers (1902-1987). He introduced humanist principles to psychotherapy and named his therapy Client Centered Psychotherapy. He shared that in the traditional psychoanalytical approach, the therapist is the authority that makes interpretations. But in Client Centered Psychotherapy the patient gains more power in the therapeutic relationship. He introduced the concept of "unconditional positive regard" in therapy.

The third humanist psychologist is Abraham Maslow (1908-1970). Maslow focused on the healthy and creative part of the human personality. He wanted to know the secret of how human beings can be inspired to become fully human. He shared his theory of a Hierarchy of Needs. He divided human needs into five groups.

1. Physiological Needs that include food, water, sleep and sex
2. Safety Needs that include security of body and health
3. Love and Belonging Needs that include friendships, family and loving relationships.
4. Esteem Needs that include self-esteem, confidence and the respect of others.
5. Self Actualizing Needs that include creativity and personal growth.

Maslow studied self-actualized people to discover how they satisfied their basic needs so that they could focus on their self-actualizing needs.

Maslow contributed not only to the field of human psychology but also to that of human spirituality. He studied spiritual and religious experiences as a psychologist and called them *peak experiences.* He believed that human beings can have *peak experiences* even if they do not have any belief in God or Religion.

The fourth humanist psychologist is Victor Frankl. After spending many years in concentration camps and losing many members of his family, when he became a free man he wrote a book titled *Man's Search for Meaning.* That book became a bestseller and was translated into many languages all over the world. In that book Frankl presents his philosophy that human suffering becomes more bearable when it finds a meaning. Based on that philosophy Frankl created a therapy model that is called Logo-therapy. In Logo-therapy the therapist helps clients find their own unique meaning in life.

Humanist psychologists and philosophers broadened the scope of human psychology. They created a holistic approach to the human condition. They inspired people to discover their unique potential and then express it. Rather than focusing on the sick part of the person's personality, humanist psychologists focus on the healthy part of that personality and find ways to inspire people to lead a creative and self-actualized life.

INSIGHTS INTO HUMAN NATURE

"Your emotional life is not written in cement during childhood. You write each chapter as you go along."
Harry Stack Sullivan

Over the centuries human beings, have remained mysterious beings. In each century, different schools of thought offered a wide range of theories to solve that mystery. In the 20th century a number of psychologists and psychotherapists, scholars and philosophers, tried to understand the dynamics of human nature. Those philosophers, in their own unique ways, tried to answer the fundamental question: what is human nature? Based on their observations and experiences, readings and reflections, they presented a number of intriguing and fascinating theories. Let me share some of the theories of human nature in this essay.

Sigmund Freud believed that human beings, like animals, are born with certain instincts, and all their lives, they try to satisfy those instincts. Such satisfaction gives them pleasure. That is why he concluded that human beings are primarily pleasure seeking beings.

Freud thought that when human beings are not able to satisfy their desires, wishes and dreams to obtain pleasure, because of their inner inhibitions or social and cultural taboos, they become frustrated and angry. To deal with those frustrations human beings repress their desires through different unconscious defense mechanisms. Such defense mechanisms can cause emotional problems and neurotic conflicts. Freud believed that neurotic symptoms are caused by sexual repression. He conceptualized a hierarchy of defense mechanisms, from the most immature to the most mature.

Freud created a form of therapy called psycho-analysis which helped his patients in bringing their repressed unconscious conflicts to the conscious mind and dealing with them in a healthy way. Freud believed that by resolving those unconscious conflicts human beings could create happy and healthy lives for themselves. He believed that emotionally healthy people are able to work and love.

While Freud believed that human beings are pleasure-seeking, Alfred Adler believed human beings are power-seeking. He believed so many human beings struggle with their sense of inadequacy. They try to find ways to compensate for their feelings of inferiority. Adler stressed the importance of self-esteem in understanding human nature. He believed that we need to see human beings as indivisible beings, as they cannot be divided into parts. That is why we call them individuals. Adler also highlighted that to understand human nature we need to understand that the social aspect of the human personality is as important as the emotional aspect.

While Freud believed that human beings are primarily pleasure-seeking beings and Adler believed that human beings are primarily power-seeking beings, Carl Jung believed that human beings are primarily spiritual beings. He agreed with Freud that human beings have an unconscious mind but he disagreed that people have only a personal unconscious mind. Jung believed in a collective unconscious mind that is expressed in the art and music and folklore of a culture. He believed that people's dreams are connected with the personal as well as the collective unconscious mind. He thought that our dreams not only reflect our past but also connect us with our future dreams and ambitions. He believed that healthy people integrate different aspects of their personality. He was of the opinion that when people come to terms with their unconscious mind they become wise men and women.

While Freud believed human beings were primarily pleasure-seeking, Harry Stack Sullivan believed they were relationship-seeking. While Freud believed that anxiety was caused by intra-psychic conflicts, Sullivan believed that human beings can also experience anxiety if they are part of a conflicted relationship that does not offer security. Sullivan pursued the ideas of Adler and emphasized the importance of self-esteem in emotional problems. Sullivan believed that to help people regain their emotional health we need to help them develop positive self-esteem, self-worth and self-confidence. Sullivan also brought to our attention that while some people struggle with anxiety and depression, there are others who suffer from loneliness. He believed that many people stay in unhappy marriages and dysfunctional relationships because they do not want to be alone and lonely. For them to be in a bad relationship is better than being in no relationship. Sullivan believed that the human personality is not a fixed thing and that it keeps on evolving with time, depending upon the choices people make in their lives.

While Sullivan highlighted the significance of human relationships in the human personality, Murray Bowen focused on the family system. He believed that human health and happiness depends on the health of the family system. Healthy families play a positive role in building a healthy personality that has a sold core. Having a solid core is a reflection of the differentiated self. Such people can deal with emotional and social crises gracefully. Those who do not have a sold core in their personality are vulnerable to suffer, as they cannot cope with life dilemmas. Bowen believed that rather than focusing on individuals, mental health professionals need to help the whole family in dealing with social and emotional challenges.

While Freud focused on the early childhood of human beings, Erik Erikson focused on the whole life span. He believed that human beings face a different challenge and dilemma in each phase of their lives and their mental health depends how they resolve their dilemmas. He stressed that the issues of old age were as important as the issues of childhood. He broadened the scope of the human personality from birth to death, from cradle to grave.

While many psychologists and psychotherapists focused on the sick part of the human personality, Abraham Maslow focused on the healthy part of the human personality. He believed that to develop insights into human nature we need to understand the best rather than the worst, the most healthy rather than the most unhealthy. While Freud presented the hierarchy of defense mechanisms, Maslow presented the hierarchy of needs. He believed that the least mature people dealt with the basic needs of food, sleep and sex, while the most mature people focused on their highest needs of creativity and personal growth. He called the most mature and evolved people *self actualized people*. Maslow also focused on those human experiences that are traditionally known as religious or spiritual experiences calling them *peak experiences*. He believed that for people to have peak experiences they did not need to believe in any God or organized religion.

While Freud believed human beings are pleasure seeking, Adler believed they were power seeking, Sullivan believed they were relationship seeking, Victor Frankl believed they were meaning seeking. They have a desire to lead meaningful lives and when they cannot find meaning they suffer from ontological insecurity and existential despair. While many psychologists and psychotherapists helped their patients deal with emotional conflicts, Frankl helped them find meaning in life. He believed that human beings can endure suffering if they discover meaning in that suffering.

While Freud and Jung focused on the person, Sullivan focused on relationships, and Bowen focused on the family, Eric Fromm focused on the community and the culture people grow up in. He showed how the human personality develops differently if people grow up in a capitalist or a communist society. He believed that emotional and social dynamics are interconnected with cultural and political dynamics. Fromm believed that individual lives of human beings are intimately connected with collective lives. Fromm was a psychologist as well a sociologist. He built a bridge between the theories of Sigmund Freud and Karl Marx. He emphasized that human beings want to be free and many of them are willing to pay a heavy price for their freedom. Fromm also believed that human beings have a need to belong to a social group and have a worldview.

While many psychologists, psychiatrists and psychotherapists believed in deterministic theories and thought that genetic and early childhood factors played a significant role in personality development, existentialist Jean Paul Sartre believed that human beings did not have any fixed human nature. All human beings are condemned to be free. They are always free to make choices. Even not making a choice is making a choice. He believed that human beings do not have a fixed personality. Each relationship and each social situation that human beings encounter brings out a different side of the personality. The same person can behave very differently depending on the relationship or the social and cultural situation. Sartre believed that healthy and mature human beings take responsibility for their actions and do not blame their behavior on the past. He did not believe in the unconscious mind. He believed that when human beings are not willing to take responsibility for their behaviors they try to forget or deny realities and then justify it by saying that the undesirable aspect was repressed into the unconscious mind. Sartre believed that human personality and nature are not fixed as they change with each significant situation, dilemma and relationship depending on the choices human beings make.

When we review theories of human personality and human nature, we realize that psychologists and psychotherapists, scholars and philosophers focused on different aspects of human personality depending upon their personal and professional experiences. Some focused on the unhealthy part, while others focused on the healthy part. Some focused on how human beings can decrease their human suffering, while others focused how they can focus on their personal growth and actualize their full potential.

As we review these theories, we see that they were created to understand emotional realities and social dilemmas. We all know that human beings have been evolving over the centuries. Human beings had different dilemmas when there were one billion people on the planet, and now they have different challenges when there are seven billion human beings in the world. Children born in the social and political conditions of Asia can develop a different personality than children born in North America. The question is what parts of the human personality are universal and what parts are affected by the dynamics of the family, community and culture. Emotional problems that Freud's patients encountered in early part of the 20th century in Vienna are different than the problems of patients encountered by psychiatrists in early part of the 21st century in many parts of the world. As practicing psychologists, psychiatrists and psychotherapists, we know that young patients suffering from a hysterical conversion reaction in the 19th century Europe had different dynamics than young patients suffering from Borderline Personality Disorder in 21st century North America. Similarly, opportunities available to children of Europe and North America in their families and schools are significantly different than those provided to the children of Africa and Latin America.

All theories of human personality and human nature are genuine attempts to help humanity to deal with their existential dilemmas. They are attempts to decrease human suffering and increase human happiness. They inspire human beings to grow to their full potential and become fully human individually and collectively. As human conditions change, so do the perspectives. In every century psychologists and psychotherapists, scholars and philosophers discover new theories to understand new problems. In the 21st century we will see new theories that will address new social and cultural, economic and political challenges. As human beings evolve, so do psychological and social theories. Human nature is as fluid as human conditions. The human personality is as changeable as the emotional and social conditions. We continue to learn and grow, and we all know that learning is a life-long process. Human beings will learn and grow till the last human being in this world. Human nature is an evolving mystery.

BECOMING FULLY HUMAN

Based on my thirty years of professional experiences as a psychotherapist and personal experiences as a humanist, I have come to this gradual realization that story of human evolution is the story of the evolution of human consciousness. Over the centuries, more and more men and women are becoming aware of being human and then choosing to become fully human.

There have been so many human beings, who ask themselves,

What makes us human?

What are the differences between animals and humans?

How can we become fully human?

There have been many philosophers, psychologists and psychotherapists who have tried to answer these questions.

There are many who realize that human beings not only walk on two feet and communicate in words, but also have developed a higher level of consciousness than animals.

Animals are aware, humans are self aware.

Animals are conscious, humans are self conscious.

Animals know, humans know that they know.

Such self awareness and higher consciousness helped humans to develop science and technology, art and culture, and create highly sophisticated communities.

Charles Darwin, in his theory of evolution, proved that through natural selection, it took animals millions of years to evolve into humans. In his book *The Descent of Man* he showed how the human brain is the evolved form of the animal brain. He shared the similarities between animals' mental qualities and human mental faculties.

Based on my readings and reflections I have come to the conclusion that for human beings to become fully human, individually and collectively, they have to accept three challenges.

1. Find ways to deal with emotional problems.
2. Find the secret of personal growth
3. Find the relationship between personal growth and social evolution.

1. EMOTIONAL PROBLEMS

As a psychotherapist I am well aware that it is very difficult for people to develop their hidden potential if they are suffering from serious emotional problems. People, who struggle with different forms of mental health problems, have to find ways to deal with those problems to lead a healthy and happy life. In many cases they need professional help from doctors and nurses, psychiatrists and psychotherapists, social workers and counselors, to learn to cope with their existential dilemmas.

In the twentieth century, a number of psychiatrists, psychologists and psychotherapists including Sigmund Freud, Harry Stack Sullivan and Murray Bowen discovered effective modes of treatment to help people cope with their emotional, relationship and family problems.

2. PERSONAL GROWTH

While many psychologists and psychotherapists belonging to psychoanalytical, interpersonal and systems theory schools of thought focused on helping people cope with their emotional, relationship and family problems, there were other philosophers, psychologists and psychotherapists, belonging to existential and humanist schools, including Jean Paul Sartre and Abraham Maslow, who helped people identify their special gifts and find ways to grow to their fullest potential. It is not uncommon for ideas about personal growth to inspire people to try to be better human beings and become fully human.

Maslow believed that when people are able to satisfy their basic needs, including survival and self esteem needs, they feel free to explore their self actualizing needs and become mature, wise and creative people.

3. SOCIAL EVOLUTION

While many individual psychologists focused on personal growth and maturity, many social psychologists tried to find the connection between individuals and their communities. Sociologists like Erich Fromm and Karl Marx showed us that for more and more people to reach their fullest potential, their states need to create social and economic, religious and cultural systems that take care of the basic needs of people, including food and clothes, housing and health care, so that people can explore their higher needs and pursue their passions in science and technology, art and culture. It is very hard for people to follow their creative dreams if they feel insecure about their survival and health, safety and security.

A number of psychologists and sociologists have brought to our attention that all individuals are an integral part of their community. Families are the connecting links between individuals and their cultures through which values and traditions of one generation are passed on to the next.

When human beings develop social consciousness and become socially responsible, they develop social and economic systems that provide equal opportunities to all members of the community. Such communities respect the human rights of their members and inspire them to develop their fullest potential and become fully human individually and collectively.

Human beings in the 21st century are at a crossroads. They have a choice to regress or progress. They can create communities full of anger, prejudice and violence. They can commit collective suicide with nuclear bombs and other weapons of mass destruction or they can create loving, harmonious and peaceful communities where all members are accepted and respected, valued and cherished. They can create cultures where it becomes natural for all children to grow to their fullest potential and become fully human individually and collectively. I hope more and more human beings choose the path of peace, so that we can all grow to the next stage of human evolution and create a peaceful world together. Let me end this essay with my poem titled *peace*.

PEACE
There is inner peace and there is outer peace
There is emotional peace and there is social peace
There is religious peace and there is political peace
There is local peace and there is global peace
These are all different colors of peace
And we need all these colors
To create a rainbow of peace.

Sohail

Chapter Three

PSYCHOTHERAPY: THE ART OF HEALING AND GROWING

INTRODUCTION

Psychotherapy has remained a mystery for professionals as well as lay people as it is subtle, experiential and very difficult to explain in a logical and rational way. It is as much of an art as a science. That is why I call psychotherapy the art of healing and growth. I am quite aware that healing and growth are abstract concepts and difficult to explain in concrete terms.

In this book, we will reflect and share with you our experiences and observations as psychotherapists to give you a general idea of the whole process from the beginning to the end, and the dilemmas patients and therapists face at different stages of therapy. Our hope is that after reading this book, you have some idea as to what to expect from the therapist and what the therapist might expect from you, so that you can enter therapy with an open mind and are able to benefit from the therapeutic process.

It is the birthright of every human being to be happy and not suffer. There is no need to feel ashamed or embarrassed about seeking professional help to create a happy, healthy and peaceful lifestyle. The more you enjoy life, the more people around you will enjoy your company and the more likely you will have a happy family and exciting social life. Psychotherapy is an art that helps people to decrease their sufferings and promote their personal and social growth.

COMMON PRESENTING PROBLEMS

Over the decades I have met many patients who share in their first session, "Doctor, I am unhappy and I want to be happy. Since I do not know why I am unhappy, I do not know what to do to be happy. Can you help me?"

It is so sad that when I ask them, "For how long you have been unhappy?" many of them say, "All my life".

During my first session when I ask them about the emotional problems they have been struggling with, some of the more common answers I get are,

> "I feel anxious."
> "I have panic attacks."
> "I feel sad all the time.'
> "I have been depressed most of my life."
> "I feel very lonely."
> "I feel miserable at work."
> "I do not like myself."
> "I am unhappy in my marriage."

"I hate my family."
"I wish I was never born."
"I do not want to die but I do not want to live either."
"Life is nothing more than suffering."

These are the patients who did not have any physical illnesses. Even after investigations by their family doctor, they were told that their test results were with in the normal range. It was suggested that a psychiatrist might have a better idea as to the problem. Many of them were told, "I do not know what is wrong with you and why you are unhappy. You need to see a psychiatrist. It might be all in your head."

Sometimes people who suffer from emotional problems feel ashamed as they think they might be imagining things. I try to share with them that those emotional problems and mental illnesses are as real as physical illnesses; the difference is that they cannot be detected by blood, urine tests or x-rays. Many of the emotional problems are related to people's personalities and lifestyles and can be assessed more by personal interviews than by laboratory tests. It is as much related to the subjective meaning in life as to the objective conditions of life. In some mysterious way the physical and the mental, the subjective and the objective lives are all interconnected. In many cases, human beings who suffer emotionally do not know how to deal with their emotions. Many of them are very intelligent and find it hard to understand that their problems are emotional rather than intellectual, and it is difficult for them to analyze them rationally and logically. Emotions have their own logic like the logic of dreams. The heart has a logic that the mind does not know. It is sometimes very frustrating for people with university degrees who can fix computer problems or can build bridges, to deal with their anxiety, depression and anger because to them these feelings are not logical and rational. The more they try to understand their feelings logically, the more they feel frustrated and overwhelmed and rather than feeling better, they feel worse. In many cases it gets so bad they have a breakdown and they are unable to work or socialize, or even get out of bed. In some cases, people are brought by their dear ones to see a doctor or a psychiatrist, as their sufferings have made them emotionally paralyzed. They feel desperate but do not know what to do about it. All the things they have tried have failed. They also realized that their emotional problems are affecting the whole family. The emotional problems of one person can easily affect others in the family, at work and in the community.

FIRST INTERVIEW
Having a first interview with a psychotherapist can be a stressful experience. To make it easier for

our patients, Bette, my co-therapist, is in contact by phone with each person that is referred. She interviews them to ensure that psychotherapy will address their needs. She also provides information about the process of psychotherapy, refers them to our website or one of our books, and answers their questions to reassure them. It is a significant advantage when someone comes into therapy having read about our approach and begun the process of healing.

The first interview at our clinic usually lasts for an hour and is conducted by both of us, which helps patients to make a smoother transition from the phone to a face to face interview.

In the initial session, the patient is encouraged to share his/her struggles while I make some notes for my assessment which is sent to the referring doctor. I share with the patient that Bette is my co-therapist and if the patient joins group therapy or we invite the spouse or other family members, Bette will join me in our group, marital or family therapy sessions.

During the first interview while we listen to their life story, we focus on making the patient feel respected and accepted. At the end, I ask the person to share their theory of why they are suffering. When they finish their story, I ask them if they want to ask us any questions. We want to create an atmosphere of a dialogue. Before the patient leaves, Bette and I offer our impressions of what they have shared, highlighting their strengths. We emphasize that we admire their courage to seek therapy and take responsibility for their problems in particular and life in general.

During my assessment I keep seven factors in mind as they affect the process of therapy. These factors reflect the patient's capacity to change and grow in therapy.

1. AGE

It is my observation that young people do better in therapy as their personalities are still flexible. As people get older they have a tendency to become rigid. Some therapists do not accept patients for dynamic or intensive psychotherapy if they are in their late forties or older. In our practice we do not deny therapy because of age if an individual is motivated to change.

2. INTELLIGENCE

For people to benefit from the psychotherapy experience they have to be of average intelligence so that they can understand the process and actively participate in it. In my opinion, people with low intelligence benefit more from behavior therapy than dynamic psychotherapy.

3. PSYCHOLOGICAL SOPHISTICATION

Psychotherapy is a psychologically sophisticated process and people who are psychologically sophisticated benefit from it more. These are the people who are curious about why they feel anxious, sad or angry and what they can do to change it. People who are intelligent but not psychologically sophisticated benefit less from psychotherapy.

4. EMOTIONAL FLEXIBILITY

Since therapy creates a change in people's personality and lifestyle, emotional flexibility is important. Some patients are more flexible than others. In my experience, people with obsessive compulsive, idealistic and perfectionist personalities have a tendency to be less flexible and have a harder time engaging and changing in therapy.

5. SIGNIFICANT RELATIONSHIPS IN THE PAST

Psychotherapy takes place in the context of a significant therapeutic relationship between the patient and the therapist. People who have experienced some type of healthy significant relationship with a parent, grandparent, teacher or friend in the past are more likely to connect with the therapist and engage in the process.

6. MOTIVATION

Motivation is one of the major factors that will dictate how much an individual will benefit from therapy. The more a person is motivated the more they change, learn and grow. Those who see a therapist because their spouse, relative or probation officer insisted on it usually do not benefit that much.

7. CONNECTION WITH THE THERAPIST
The final factor that I consider significant in my assessment is the connection with the therapist. The more connected the patient feels with us and the more connected we feel with the patient, the higher the likelihood for therapy to be successful. I find it amazing that in spite of many social, linguistic and cultural differences, most patients feel connected and are inspired to work with us.

WORKING THROUGH THE PROBLEMS
Most patients we see do their major work in a year. They start to see me weekly for an hour for a few months and when they join the group psychotherapy sessions their individual sessions become less frequent. We tailor therapy according to the individual's needs. Many are involved in a combination of individual, marital or group therapy sessions. Some also may have family therapy sessions. It is our goal that our patients create and maintain healthy relationships.

SPOKEN AND WRITTEN WORDS
Psychotherapy is generally known as the *talking cure*. The psychotherapist and patient use words to share their thoughts and feelings, and such exchanges have a therapeutic effect on the patient.

Over a period of time, new and old emotional wounds heal and the patient grows as a person.

Being a poet and a writer I have also discovered the power of written words. That is why I encourage my patients to keep a diary or write letters highlighting their progress in therapy. I feel that therapy does not happen only during therapy sessions, it also happens during the time between the sessions. Many times patients develop an insight or a realization that is significant in therapy and if they do not record it, they forget it. So I ask them to keep a regular diary and bring it with them when they come for their sessions. When they bring out their diary and read parts of it in the sessions, they have an opportunity to discuss and explore some of their experiences and their reactions that took place in between the sessions.

As a therapist and a writer, I am fascinated with the healing power of words. Just in the last few months, two of my patients who were in the early stages of therapy developed the courage to verbalize their truth in a few powerful words. A fifty year old man, for the first time in his life, said in group therapy, "I am gay", while a fifty-year-old woman, also for the first time in her life, said in her individual session, "I was raped". Saying those three words was a turning point in their therapy. They felt comfortable enough in therapy to share their truth without worrying about being judged, humiliated or made fun of. In therapy when the therapist or other group members accept and respect them, that helps them in turn to accept and respect themselves.

As therapy progresses, patients are able to share their deeper secrets and wounds that have been hurting them for years. They share their story of their sufferings and as they heal, they develop more self-confidence and self-worth and improve their self-image. As their self-esteem improves they are able to grow and explore their fullest potential.

One of the realities people discover in therapy is that the process of healing and growing is complex. The recovery is not linear. People take three steps forward and one step back. Sometimes when they take a step backwards they feel discouraged. That is the time I ask them to read their diary to see that even when they have taken a step backwards, they are still farther ahead of the beginning point from which they started their journey. I also share with them the analogy that when a car is stuck in the snow, sometimes we have to drive backwards and then forwards. Moving backwards and forwards helps to get unstuck.

Many people in therapy realize that having grown up in unhealthy families and communities, they have learnt some unhealthy and self-destructive patterns. Group therapy provides them with an opportunity to become aware of such patterns and then break them so that they learn new and healthier patterns. In many cases such a process is slow and needs a lot of patience and endurance. Group therapy is effective in the way that the healing and growth of one person offers hope and inspiration to another person to keep on coming and working in therapy. Some people have to strike 99 times before the rock breaks at the 100th strike. When the rock breaks, the person realizes that the 99 previous strikes were not wasted.

In therapy people realize that their emotional crisis, while painful, was also an opportunity to grow. Many told me that after therapy they reached a higher level of growth than they had before the crisis. So therapy did not just help them to heal, it also helped them to grow further towards their fullest potential. Many said, "I was living at 6 out of 10 before therapy. During the crisis I dropped to 3. And now after therapy, I am living at 8 out of 10."

When people heal and recover I ask them to decrease the frequency of appointments and move from active therapy to maintenance therapy. I reassure them that the door to our clinic is always open. I jokingly say that our clinic might have a long waiting list but it offers a life-long membership. Some of our patients come just once or twice a year to share their progress and growth and their successes in life. Others come back to attend group therapy as guest patients and share their success story to inspire new members. Some of them write and volunteer their success stories and we add them to our website for others to read.

END OF THERAPY

There comes a time when a person is ready to say goodbye to us, to therapy and to our clinic, as they feel healed and confident to deal with the dilemmas of life on their own. At that time, I sometimes share with them a letter I received from my therapist colleague who was in therapy herself and had written that letter for her therapist. I thought it was a wonderful gift for a therapist as it reflects the mysterious but meaningful relationship between patient and the therapist. Let me end this chapter by sharing that letter with you.

LAST LETTER TO A THERAPIST

There was a small and old book. It was in a corner on a shelf in the library. Most of its pages were glued together, a few of them were torn. The cover was stained and one couldn't read the writer's name. No one knew its content. Sometimes people would glance at it but not bother to pick it up. Some would pick it up and promptly put it back in its place, while others would get curious about the writer's name but after useless efforts would give up.

One day you stepped into the library, you looked at the book, you turned it a few times trying to understand its origin, and to decipher the writer's name. You decided to discover its content. You took all the tools you had. You used all the tools you needed: water, a lot of water, pins, needles, threads, brushes. You related to every page like it was a masterpiece, you washed the glue, you let it dry, you added the missing words and only when the pages were complete did you put them in the original order, and you sewed one to the other. At the same time you were absorbed reading the story, paying attention to every simple word because every word was important to you. You were attracted by the big facts and by the small nuances as well. You learned the story and it had a big value for you. You understood its value. Now the book is complete, the story clear, with a beginning and an end. Now the book is ready to be read by the other people too.

Lois

Chapter Four

DR. WOLF AND THE MIRACLE OF A HEALING RELATIONSHIP

When I started my psychiatric residency at Memorial University of Newfoundland in 1977, I had an intellectually stimulating opportunity to work with many renowned professors. Some focused on psychopharmacology, others on behavior therapy, while a few had developed an expertise in psychotherapy. I learnt from all of them but I came particularly close to Dr. Eugene Wolf, a visiting professor of psychotherapy from England.

One day Dr. Wolf announced that he wanted to offer group therapy sessions and needed one resident to join him as a co-therapist. I was the most junior resident but I was the one most motivated to become a psychotherapist, so I approached Dr. Wolf. I was surprised that none of the other residents showed any interest in group psychotherapy. Dr. Wolf accepted me as his assistant and I was thrilled.

I remember the first time Dr. Wolf met with the residents. He told us that he had been approached by an internist to see a new patient in the Intensive Care Unit who had been admitted after a suicide attempt. Dr. Wolf suggested that he would like to interview the patient in front of the residents. We all agreed.

A tall heavyset man with red hair and a beard was brought by the nurse. Dr. Wolf got up, introduced himself, shook hands and asked the patient, Bill, to sit beside him. Bill was very reserved. When Dr. Wolf asked him what had brought him to the hospital, he shared that he was a pharmacist and had calculated the exact dose of medications to kill himself. One afternoon when his wife Sheila had arranged to go away for the weekend to see her sister, he had planned to take an overdose. Sheila left at 5pm and he took the overdose at 5:30. Unexpectedly, Sheila returned in the evening as she had forgotten her purse and found him unconscious in his bed. She called the ambulance and he was brought to the Emergency Department. His stomach was pumped and he was admitted to the Intensive Care Unit to be seen by a psychiatrist.

When Dr. Wolf asked him why he wanted to kill himself, he shared that his life was a complete failure and one of the proofs he offered was that even his suicide attempt was a failure. Bill told us that some people think that committing suicide is an irrational act but he believed that he had analyzed his life logically and that his decision to kill himself was a rational choice as he had no reason to live.

When Dr. Wolf inquired about his wife, he stated that they had been married for twenty years and he believed that his wife did not love him anymore. He thought that she was staying with him out of pity as she felt sorry for him. She had not told him she loved him in years and he was in a sexless and loveless marriage.

At the end of the session, Dr. Wolf offered a therapeutic contract with him in which he would promise not to commit suicide for six months and would see Dr. Wolf for weekly individual, marital and group therapy sessions. Bill thought for the longest time and finally accepted Dr. Wolf's invitation, saying, "I have to die anyhow. I can wait for another few months."

I was impressed by the way Dr. Wolf interviewed the patient and asked if he could attend the six months of psychotherapy sessions. I thought if Dr. Wolf could save his life, it would be a miracle.

When I met with Dr. Wolf alone he shared his philosophy. I learnt that he was an admirer of Harry Stack Sullivan, an American psychiatrist who was the founder of interpersonal psychiatry in North America. Sullivan believed that human relationships are a great source of anxiety, depression and low self esteem; and it is a caring and compassionate relationship that is healing. Dr. Wolf believed that human beings commit suicide when they lose all their special connections with other human beings, and then even one loving connection is enough to prevent suicide. Dr. Wolf was planning to offer Bill a caring therapeutic relationship and explore his relationship with his wife.

When Bill and Sheila got involved in therapy we found out more about them as individuals and about their relationship. Bill told us that when he was only two, his mother had died giving birth to another child. His father remarried when he was three but his stepmother was very abusive as she was jealous of Bill's relationship with his father. Finally Bill was sent when he was five to live with his grandmother. His grandmother died of a stroke when he was ten and he came back to stay with his father and step-mother. When he was a teenager, he went to live in the college hostel and never returned home. Dr. Wolf thought that Bill had been deprived of nurturing and a mother's love. He had found a refuge in rationalization and intellectualization, and had difficulties connecting with others at an emotional level. He had met his wife at university and both of them enjoyed discussing philosophy and science. Their love was intellectual love. Sheila, on the other hand, was brought up in a family where her brother had died two years before her birth. Her father wanted a son, so when Sheila was born, she was treated as a boy and she grew up to be a tomboy. Her father used to dress her up like a boy and take her to his business meetings wherever he went. Sheila became an intellectual, did a Masters in Science and had become a science teacher. She was a matter-of-fact person and rarely focused on her feelings. When she met Bill in university she was glad to find someone who was as interested in abstract thinking as she was.

When Dr. Wolf interviewed Sheila, she was shocked to find out that Bill thought she did not love him. When Sheila asked what she could do to help Bill, Dr. Wolf suggested, "For a few months rather than starting your sentence with "I think" you should start it with "I feel". He helped Sheila to see that Bill needed a strong emotional connection to live and thrive. He wanted her to nurture him. Sheila was quite pleased with her interview.

In the next few months, Dr. Wolf suggested to the couple that they have weekly dates, go out for dinners, movies and dances, and plan some romantic encounters. It was amazing to see Bill smile and laugh and respond to Sheila emotionally and romantically.

After six months when Dr. Wolf interviewed Bill again in front of the residents, Bill thanked him for giving him a new life. Dr. Wolf believed it was not his miracle, it was the miracle of a healing relationship. After that encounter with Dr. Wolf and Bill, I wondered whether I would be able to help suicidal patients and perform such healing miracles when I became a practicing psychotherapist.

When the satisfaction or the security of another person becomes as significant to one as one's own satisfaction or security, then the state of love exists. Under no other circumstances is a state of love present, regardless of the popular usage of the term.

Harry Stack Sullivan

Chapter Five

QUALITIES OF SUCCESSFUL THERAPISTS

I received one of the biggest surprises of my professional life during my first week of psychiatric residency at Memorial University Newfoundland. When our professor asked the residents why they had chosen psychiatry, I was shocked to learn that many were there by default. They had wanted to become internists and surgeons but they had not been accepted in their desired field of specialization and since there was a seat available in psychiatry, they chose to become psychiatrists. I could not imagine joining a profession about which I did not feel passionate. I shared with the professor and my classmates that I wanted to become a psychotherapist because I was fascinated with the mysteries of the mind and I wanted to help my patients deal with their emotional problems so that they could lead happy, healthy and peaceful lives.

During my student life while I was studying different schools of human psychology and psychotherapy, I was also curious about the qualities of successful psychotherapists. Of all the psychologists and psychotherapists that I studied, I found two who had wonderful ideas about how to become a good psychotherapist: Frieda Fromm Reichmann and Anna Freud. One of the reasons I focused on these two is that many students of psychotherapy do not acknowledge and appreciate the contributions of female psychotherapists.

Frieda Fromm Reichmann was a well-respected psychoanalyst. She not only admired Sigmund Freud's ideas but also challenged his philosophy. She broadened the therapeutic horizons of psychoanalysis by including the philosophical and psychological insights of Harry Stack Sullivan.

While Freud focused on the treatment of neurotics, Reichmann also included psychotics in her clinical practice. She looked after many patients suffering from schizophrenia who were admitted to psychiatric hospitals. She not only identified their special needs but also found special techniques to serve them. Rather than expecting patients to fit into the strict discipline of psychoanalysis, she modified her therapy practice to accommodate them and serve them better. For example, rather than requiring patients to have hourly sessions every day, she saw some of them for half an hour two or three times a week because such individuals could handle only that much time in therapy.

Reichmann was a wonderful teacher. Based on her many lectures to her students, she wrote a book *Principles of Intensive Psychotherapy*, which is a goldmine for mental health professionals. In that book she focuses not only on the therapeutic process but also on the personality of the psychotherapist. She believes that for therapists to become effective and successful they need to develop certain characteristics and have a certain lifestyle.

1. GOOD LISTENERS

Good therapists need to have an ability to listen. For therapists to listen to their patients they need to pay attention to verbal as well as nonverbal behavior. They need to attend not only what they are saying but also to what they are trying to say. They need to pay attention not only to behavior but also change of behavior because non-verbal behaviors and changes of behaviors can be quite meaningful in therapy. When patients realize that their therapists are listening to them attentively, they not only feel special but also develop a trusting relationship with their therapist which acts as the foundation of a healing relationship.

2. RESPECTING PATIENTS

Good therapists need to respect their patients. They need to believe that all human beings have more similarities than differences because they are human. Therapists are different from their patients only because they have acquired certain knowledge, experience and wisdom to help people with emotional problems.

Reichmann believed that therapists are similar not only to their neurotic patients but also to their psychotic patients. She believed that what therapists experience in their dreams at night with their eyes closed, psychotic patients experience during the day with their eyes wide open. To understand dreams and psychotic experiences we need different logic than the logic of solving day-to-day problems of life.

3. SEXUAL SATISFACTION

Good therapists need to have personal lives that satisfy their sexual needs. They need to have accepted their sexuality and created healthy sexual relationships with their partners so that they are not vulnerable to seeking sexual satisfaction through their interactions with their patients. Even when needy patients approach them sexually, experienced therapists are able to set healthy boundaries. They teach their patients that sexual contacts between a patient and a therapist are inappropriate and detrimental to their healing in therapy. Good therapists provide a trusting and respectful relationship to their patients so that they can share their sexual vulnerabilities without worrying that their therapist would manipulate or exploit their weaknesses.

4. NEED FOR SLEEP

Therapists need to have regular sleeping hours and feel fully rested when they come to their clinics or hospitals, so that they are able to pay full attention to their patients. When therapists are tired and exhausted, they are not fully present in their therapy sessions. Such an interaction can undermine the trusting relationship between patient and therapist. Some of my patients have told me that their previous therapist dozed off during therapy sessions because they were tired. Such patients were so disappointed in their therapists that they never went back. Some of them felt guilty that they were so boring that they could not keep their therapists engaged in a lively dialogue.

5. OVERCOMING LONELINESS

Therapists need to have an active social life so that they look after their interpersonal needs outside the clinic. Therapists who are very shy, introverted and lonely are vulnerable to using their relationship with their clients to satisfy their social needs. I have met a number of therapists who lived alone and felt very lonely as they did not have a circle of close friends. In some cases their clients became part of their social circle and created complications in their personal as well as professional lives.

6. FEELING SECURE

Therapists need to feel secure in their hearts and minds to become good therapists. They need to have high self-esteem to feel confident in their personal and professional lives. Their self-confidence helps their patients to build their own self-confidence as many patients see their therapists as their mentors and role models. When therapists lack confidence, their patients feel insecure in their presence and find it difficult to become successful in their lives. When patients experience a crisis or a breakdown they need to feel secure that their therapist will support them to recover and then guide them to transform their breakdown into a breakthrough.

7. DEALING WITH HOSTILE FEELINGS

Therapists need to feel secure enough in themselves that they can deal with angry and hostile reactions in their patients. Many patients bring their anger with their parents and spouses to therapy. Their anger towards their therapist can be a displaced anger. Experienced therapists recognize the transference reactions and reflect on their own counter-transference so that they do not take their patients' anger personally. They respond to this anger in a kind, caring and compassionate way so that patients can process it in the safe environment of a therapeutic relationship. Gradually patients realize that their anger was a displaced anger. Freud used to say that therapy provides a "corrective emotional experience" to patients—it allows them to vent their feelings and then let go of past hostilities. Such an exchange has a therapeutic effect.

A therapist who feels secure as a person and a therapist feels comfortable admitting their flaws and limitations. Such acknowledgment helps patients see their therapists in a more realistic way and accept them as human. Therapists' humility increases respect in the eyes of their patients.

8. RESPECTING PATIENTS' ETHICAL AND CULTURAL VALUES

When therapists see patients from diverse cultural backgrounds, it is not uncommon for them and those they serve to have different cultural and ethical values. Good therapists acknowledge those differences and do not let them become hurdles in therapy. Good therapists know that they are there to help their patients and not to impress them. Sigmund Freud once said, "The psychoanalyst's job is to help the patient, not to demonstrate how clever the doctor is."

Being an Eastern therapist who looks after Western patients, I face many cultural differences with my patients. I share with them that I learn many things from them from a cultural point of view while they learn things from me from a professional point of view. I see cultural, religious and gender differences in therapy as a blessing rather than a curse. I believe such differences enrich the therapeutic process. It helps therapists and well as patients develop a multicultural personality and see life from different points of view. Such a dialogue is very informative as well as growth-promoting.

When Anna Freud was asked about the characteristics of good psychotherapists she identified the following qualities.

9. LOVE FOR TRUTH
Good therapists need to be in love with truth. She identified two kinds of truth.
Scientific truth that is objective truth
Personal truth that is subjective truth
To learn the art and science of psychotherapy, therapists need to be in love with both truths and be able to accept those truths even when they do not feel comfortable with them.

Therapy passes through different phases and at each phase therapists as well as patients discover new insights about themselves and about each other. Such insights also help to develop hind-sights and foresights. When therapists and patients embrace those insights they can make positive changes in their lives, and therapists and patients not only grow individually but also grow together. Therapy becomes a growth-promoting encounter for both parties.

10. WIDE RANGE OF INTERESTS

Anna Freud believed that good therapists need to have a wide range of interests. They need to have strong interest in literature and philosophy, art and culture. She believed that good therapists are interested not only in patients' emotional problems but also their social, religious and cultural lives so that they can help their patents make wise choices in life. She believed that literature offers many wonderful insights into the human condition that therapists can use in their clinical practice.

To become good therapists I suggest to my students that they study not only the philosophies but also the biographies of different psychologists and psychotherapists so that they develop an appreciation for their personal challenges and the sacrifices they had to make to fulfill their dream of becoming good psychotherapists.

I remember meeting an examiner of the Royal College of Physicians and Surgeons of Canada during dinner at a psychiatric conference. I asked him, "After your interview with a student is over, how you decide whether you are going to pass or fail that candidate?"

The examiner smiled and said, "I ask myself one question."

"And what is that million-dollar question that helps you decide whether someone will become a psychiatrist or not?" I was curious.

"I ask myself, 'If my mother was suffering from depression, would I send her to see this therapist?' If the answer is 'yes', I pass the candidate, and if the answer is 'no', I fail the candidate."

Good therapists generate feelings of trust and confidence in their patients and their families.

Chapter Six

GREEN ZONE THERAPY

Over the decades I have realized that there are so many people all around us who silently suffer all their lives and not even their close friends and family members know the intensity of their emotional pain. It is partly because there is so much social stigma against mental illness that many people suffering from emotional problems feel ashamed and embarrassed to share their troubles with others. It is easier for people to publicly acknowledge that they suffer from physical problems, whether hypertension or diabetes, cirrhosis or cancer and find that others are sympathetic, but it is very difficult for people to acknowledge to others that they suffer from anxiety or depression, schizophrenia or bipolar disorder, marital problems or addictions because they are afraid that people will judge them and then ostracize them. It is sad that many never get professional or social help and suffer in silence.

After working in psychiatric hospitals, general hospitals and mental health clinics for years, I chose to start a psychotherapy clinic to develop a self-help program for my patients and their families. I wanted people with emotional problems to have a better understanding of their suffering and better ways to discover a healthy, happy and peaceful lifestyle. I felt that when people had physical problems their doctors made suggestions about their diet and exercise so that they could help themselves, but when they suffered from emotional problems they sent them to psychiatrists to get medications but did not guide them to improve their quality of life. In my opinion, medications were the last step and not the first step to deal with emotional problems. I wanted to help people by educating them about the dynamics of their emotional suffering so that they could learn skills to help themselves and their dear ones. I wanted them to learn that a crisis can be an opportunity to grow and feel optimistic, and that breakdowns could be transformed into breakthroughs. Finally with the help of my patients and my colleagues, Anne Henderson and Bette Davis, I was successful in creating a self-help program called Green Zone Living based on the Green Zone Philosophy.

In the last ten years we have published five books and produced two videos to help our patients and their families. We have written them in easy to understand language and included the stories of our patients. The books in the Green Zone Series include:

1. *The Art of Living in your Green Zone*
2. *The Art of Loving in your Green Zone*

3. The Art of Working in your Green Zone
4. Creating Green Zone Schools - The Art of Learning in your Green Zone, and
5. Green Zone Living - 7 Steps to a healthy, happy and peaceful lifestyle.
6. From Breakdowns to Breakthroughs-Stories of Green Zone Therapy.

The videos are:
1.   *Green Zone Stories, and*
2.   *Green Zone Lifestyles.*

These books and videos have helped numerous people by providing them hope and inspiration and teaching them life and social skills.

In this chapter I would like to discuss the basic ideas and concepts of the Green Zone Philosophy that is the foundation of this self-help program and Green Zone Therapy. Green Zone Philosophy was conceived and delivered in the Creative Psychotherapy Clinic which became its labor room.

I feel honored that my patients trusted me with their stories and gave me an opportunity to serve them. I learnt as much from them as they learnt from me. I would not have been able to create this Green Zone Philosophy if they had not been my co-travelers on this professional journey.

GIVING BIRTH TO GREEN ZONE PHILOSOPHY
Being a creative person I am used to experiencing a wide range of creative moments, some minor,

some major, some ordinary, some extraordinary, some simple, some profound. For me, they are all precious as they help me in developing insights into my personal, social and professional life. Those profoundly creative moments are associated with "aha" experiences. Those moments are special gifts as they change and transform my life and inspire me to grow. I remember experiencing one of those profoundly creative moments a few years ago during a psychotherapy session with a couple. I was most concerned about the episodes of domestic violence. Nancy, the wife shared with me that Bill, her husband of twenty years, verbally and physically abused her. She had given him an ultimatum, to get professional help or she would leave and file for divorce. Bill did not want to lose her so he agreed to see a doctor. Their family doctor referred the couple to me as he had previously sent many couples to my clinic.

In the first couple of sessions I made an assessment of the dynamics of the relationship and tried to connect with the couple. It seemed as if the husband was genuinely interested in changing but did not know how. He had had poor role models as a child and had grown up in an unhappy family where his father was abusive to his mother.

Bill and Nancy had a 12-year-old son. In the third session, Bill told me that he loved his son and called him "Prince". When I asked him, "Do you want to see your son become a prince?" he said, "Yes". I smiled and responded, "If you want your son to be a prince, then you have to treat his mother like a queen. If you treat her like a slave, he will never be a prince." Bill smiled and that smile connected us. He realized that I was compassionate and was trying to help him.

In the next session I gently confronted him by asking, "How can you hurt the woman you love?" He seemed apologetic and said, "Dr. Sohail, I do not know what happens that I get triggered and lose control. I say and do things that I regret the next day. I apologize but after a few days I do the same thing all over again."

While I was listening to him, I looked into his eyes and said, "Bill, listen to me carefully. When you are driving and you see a yellow light, what do you do?"

"I put my foot on the accelerator."

"And why is that?"

"I am always in a hurry, in a hurry to go to work, and in a hurry to get home."

"Bill, when a wise man sees a yellow light, he puts his foot on the brake and not on the accelerator. A wise man stops, and goes forward only when there is a green light. When you are angry, you are in the Yellow Zone. You need to stop and wait and go forward only when you are in a relaxed and peaceful Green Zone, otherwise you will lose control and fall into the toxic Red Zone."

The next week when Nancy came she was thrilled.

"What did you do, Dr. Sohail? What did you say to Bill? You have performed a miracle. He is a changed man. He has not lost control in a whole week. I am so impressed."

I realized that Bill was ready to change, and his love for Nancy and his trusting relationship with me helped make that change possible.

I contemplated that change and realized that the image of the Green, Yellow and Red traffic lights had a powerful potential. It was visual. It was effective. It helped people to develop self-awareness as well as self-control. I shared the concept with other couples and found it very helpful. That concept was the seed that grew in my mind and over the years, became a plant, then a tall tree which started bearing fruits. Those fruits are the series of concepts inter-linked in the Green Zone Philosophy. Such a philosophy has become the foundation of the Self-Help program named Green Zone Living that Bette and I use in our personal lives as well as in Green Zone Therapy that we practice in our professional life. Discovering and practicing Green Zone Philosophy has made our lives and the lives of many of our patients, colleagues and friends quite peaceful. It is our gift to suffering humanity that helps people heal and grow and develop their fullest potential. Green Zone Philosophy helps us discover our inner peace and then join others to create peaceful relationships, families, workplaces and communities. I will share some of the basic concepts and principles of Green Zone Philosophy and Green Zone Therapy in the following pages.

3 EMOTIONAL ZONES - GREEN, YELLOW, RED
Green, Yellow and Red Zones are three imaginary Emotional Zones. The basic concept is that, like the traffic lights, all of us live in one of these three zones. When we are relaxed and happy and enjoying life, we are in our Green Zone, and when we are mildly sad, frustrated and unhappy, we are in our Yellow Zone. When we get depressed, angry, lose control and become irrational, we are in our Red Zone. I am of the opinion that the awareness of our Emotional Zones is the first step towards improving our mental health and creating a healthy, happy and peaceful life that I call Green Zone Living.

The Green Zone concept is simple but multifaceted. When I say the Green Zone concept is simple, I mean it can be understood by children. Let me share a story with you. One day my poet friend, Rasheed Nadeem called to share with me that his 5-year-old daughter, Afroze and 7-year-old son, Imroze were fighting. Afroze was crying. When Nadeem went into the room to help them, Afroze said, "Dad, you go back to the living room. I cannot talk to you. I am in my Red Zone." After a few minutes she came to him and said, "Dad, I am in my Yellow Zone. I can talk how." When Nadeem asked her what had pushed her to the Red Zone, she told him that her brother had broken her doll. When Nadeem asked her how he could help, she said, "Dad, if you promise to buy me a new doll, I will come to the Green Zone, but if you do not promise, I will go back to my Red Zone." Nadeem laughed, gave her a big hug and promised to buy a new doll. Nadeem told me that his children use that model all the time, although sometimes to their advantage.

At the same time, the Green Zone Model is so multifaceted that our colleague Rufi who is a manager has incorporated it into his workplace. He has bought 60 Green, Yellow and Red flags for his 60 employees in their offices. They put the flag in an obvious place to let other people know what Zone they are in. During the day, when a staff member's mood changes, the flag changes. It helps colleagues to decide when they should approach others. When Rufi's boss was visiting from Los Angeles, he was quite impressed by those flags and suggested that he would like to introduce the Green Zone Model to their head office in America.

3 Rs: RECOGNIZING, RECOVERING, RESTRAINING

I share with my patients that one of the most significant principles of Green Zone Philosophy is that the more aware we are of the changes in our Emotional Zones, the more able we are to control them and spend more time in our peaceful Green Zone. The concept of 3Rs puts that principle into action.

- The first R is Recognizing the changes in our Emotional Zones.
- The second R is Recovering from our Yellow and Red Zones.
- The third R is Restraining from going back to our Yellow and Red Zones.

The more aware people are of their emotional triggers, the better they can deal with them and learn skills to avoid being affected by them. They learn that Green Zone people *ACT* while Red Zone people *REACT* in life.

I also bring to people's attention that their self-esteem plays a key role in their mental health. People with poor self-esteem are more vulnerable to suffer as they may be overly sensitive to other people's comments and criticisms.

Of all the psychologists and philosophers who discussed the issue of self-esteem, the one who impressed me the most was Harry Stack Sullivan, an American psychiatrist, who was one of the pioneers of the interpersonal school of psychiatry. He believed that poor self-esteem was the corner stone of all emotional problems.

He developed the concept of *Good Me* and *Bad Me.* He believed that all those things that we like about ourselves are part of *Good Me* and all those things that we do not like about ourselves is part of *Bad Me*. For emotionally healthy people, Good Me is far bigger than Bad Me and in people with emotional problems, Bad Me is far bigger than Good Me. We need to help people with emotional problems make their Good Me bigger than their Bad Me. This can be done by helping them focus on their potentials, talents and their natural gifts to improve their self-esteem, self-worth and self-confidence.

People with poor self-esteem are more vulnerable to being emotionally triggered by internal and external stimuli and then reacting to stressors.

I have developed the concept of *other esteem* as compared to self-esteem. Self-esteem is the esteem that we develop ourselves, and other esteem is the esteem that we rely on others to give us. People who rely on other esteem more than self-esteem are more vulnerable to be emotionally triggered and go to their Yellow and Red Zones because they are sensitive to the negative comments of their friends, colleagues and family members. On the other hand, people whose esteem is not dependent on others and who can create their own esteem feel more secure and are less affected by the negative comments of others.

3 WAYS TO DEAL WITH CONFLICTS: RESOLVE, DISSOLVE, MEDIATE

After spending more and more time in our peaceful Green Zone, we can focus on our relationships. I ask people that I work with to make a list of all their significant relationships and then decide which Zone each relationship is in. The relationships that live in the Yellow and Red Zones can be brought to the Green Zone if we discuss those issues with our dear ones. We can approach them suggesting that we can deal with our conflicts in three ways.

The first way is to *resolve* the conflicts by improving the quality of communication.

The second way is to *dissolve* the relationship and say goodbye to that person.

But if we do not want to dissolve the relationship we can suggest a mediator, whether a friend, a relative or a therapist that both parties respect, to assist in resolving the relationship issues. Resolving, dissolving and mediating can save most relationships and increase the amount of time spent in the Green Zone.

One of the significant principles of Green Zone Philosophy is that Green Zone communication takes place when both parties are in the Green Zone. I share with my patients that there are Green Zone words that help communication and Red Zone words that hinder communication.

Let me share an example. One spouse leaves the office and gets stuck in traffic and reaches home late while the other spouse is waiting after cooking dinner. As he enters the house he says," I am sorry, I am late. I got stuck in traffic." Rather than being sympathetic she says, "You are *always* late" and he replies, "You are *never* sympathetic." *Always* and *never* are Red Zone words. Similarly, *Should* is a Red Zone word. It makes the other person feel like a child and Adult to Adult communication changes to Parent-Child communication. The interaction can easily fall into the Red Zone as one person feels criticized by the other.

On the other hand, asking people what they would like to do, want to do and love to do keeps the relationship and communication in the Green Zone as these words are Green Zone words. Similarly affectionate words like *honey, sweetheart, my love,* are Green Zone words as they keep the relationship and communication in a loving and peaceful space.

3 SYSTEMS: FAMILY, WORK, COMMUNITY

After dealing with relationships, we can focus on the social systems that we live in. There are three that are the most important: Family, Work and Community. Like people and relationships, systems also live in Green, Yellow and Red Zones. Recognizing what Zone our systems live in prompts us to consider not only what we want to do to change them but how we can buffer ourselves when we enter them. Dealing with systems is particularly challenging, as systems are often emotionally stronger than individuals because we are out numbered. But evaluating our systems and making healthy changes are vital components of living in our Green Zone since it is hard to live in the Green Zone if your major systems are in the Red.

In our book, *The Art of Working in Your Green Zone*, Bette and I discuss how employees can transform a work environment from the Red Zone to the Green Zone or leave a toxic Red Zone to join a peaceful, healthy Green Zone workplace.

DISCOVERING OUR SPECIAL GIFT

Discovering our special gift is an integral part of Green Zone Philosophy. In my clinical practice, I meet so many people who have lost the connection with their dreams. They look and feel sad. When I review their lives, I find out that they have no goals, no ambitions, no ideals, no passions and no dreams. They do not live, they just exist. As I get to know them and hear their stories, I discover that they had dreams as teenagers, but as they grew older, they lost their dreams along the way.

After finishing school, they started looking for a job, got married, had children and got so involved in their day-to-day responsibilities that their lives became monotonous and boring. Their lives became too much work and too little play. When they came to see me, they realized they not only had lost their dreams but were also losing their hope. One woman said, "My future is a blank slate. I do not see anything."

I share with such people that all of us are born with a special gift and discovering that special gift is half of the struggle. Once we discover it then we need to nurture it so that it can grow to its fullest potential. Fortunate are those children who have parents and grandparents, aunts and uncles, teachers and principals, who pay special attention to them and recognize their talent and potential before they recognize it themselves.

My poet uncle Arif told me that his aunt used to tell him, "The way you sit and hold your chin on your palm and stare into space in deep thought, you will become a philosopher one day." My uncle was lucky to have such an aunt and I was lucky to have an uncle who nurtured my creativity and inspired me to become an artist, a humanist and a psychotherapist.

But what about all those people who did not have such nurturing and inspiring adults in their life? I believe we can discover our talent and special gifts even as adults, sometimes on our own, sometimes with the support of friends, and sometimes with the encouragement of therapists. Green Zone Therapy helps in that creative journey.

3 PARTS THE OF SELF : NATURAL, CONDITIONED AND CREATIVE

The first part of the self is our *Natural Self* that we are all born with. Like the seed of a plant, all the potential is hidden in that seed. If that seed is nurtured then it grows to be a plant or a tree and bears fruit. Like a plant needs fresh air, rain and sunshine to grow, children need caring, love and discipline to become healthy adults who can not only work but also play. They find a balance in their lives and grow to their fullest potential.

Over time our Natural Self transforms into the second and third parts, the *Conditioned Self* and *Creative Self*. The Conditioned Self develops as a result of social, religious and cultural conditioning by our families and communities. This part of the Self is guided by *should, have to* and *must*. That is the part that helps us be responsible and carry on family and community traditions. On the other hand, the Creative Self develops when we follow our desires, wishes and ambitions. Such a part is guided by what we *like to, want to* and *love to do*.

Healthy, happy and peaceful people have found a balance between their Conditioned and Creative Self. Many people that we meet in our clinical practice have an overdeveloped Conditioned Self and an underdeveloped Creative Self. That is why they feel anxious, depressed and angry as their lives are guided by many *shoulds.* To develop their Creative Self, I suggest that they find an hour a day, a Green Zone Hour, in which they do what they love to do. That is the beginning of a hobby, and with the passage of time, that hobby becomes their passion and then transforms into a dream. Their lives become more enjoyable and meaningful. When I think of all the people who nurtured their Creative Self, I remember:

- a man who became a photographer,
- a woman who became a gardener,
- another woman who became an expert in stained glass,
-another man who became an accomplished musician, and
- many who became inspiring writers.

3 ROADS TO A GREEN ZONE LIFESTYLE: CREATING, SHARING AND SERVING

I share with the people I work with, that after learning to have a Green Zone Day and a Green Zone Week, if they want to further pursue the Green Zone Philosophy to create a Green Zone Lifestyle they need to follow three roads.

The first road is of *Creating* which they follow by developing their Creative Self. They create things that they enjoy.

The second road is of *Sharing*. After they have developed their creations, I ask them to share their creations with others and create a circle of friends, that I call the *Family of the Heart*. In that process, they make new friends and develop meaningful relationships with people who have similar interests, passions and dreams. For me, it is the circle of my writer friends. We meet every week in a small group and every month in a big group. Each month we invite new members. Through the Internet we are connected with a very large group who stay in touch with us and read our creations.

The third road is *Serving*. After *Creating* and *Sharing* with close friends, I ask people to do some volunteer work to contribute to their communities. I feel that Green Zone people are well connected with their communities and serve them to become part of creating Green Zone Communities. Some like to lead and become Green Zone leaders, while others like to follow and become part of the team. Some have their own dream and some join others in their dreams. Sometimes Green Zone people are able to create healthy and peaceful Green Zone islands in dysfunctional and toxic Red Zone seas, whether in the family, at work or in the community. When people start to recognize and appreciate their sincere efforts to create Green Zone Communities they join them and those islands become bigger and bigger. More and more people have the courage and strength to change their lives and transform the breakdowns of their families and communities into breakthroughs. They become part of creating a peaceful Green Zone World together.

At the end of therapy people recognize the essence of the Green Zone Philosophy. They realize that Green Zone Living is peaceful living. It starts with inner peace and ends in outer peace.

People realize that emotional and social, political and cultural, national and international peace, are all connected in a mysterious way. Gradually, people learn to act locally and think globally. They develop a Green Zone relationship not only with their own families and communities, but with all of humanity and discover unity in diversity.

To make it easier for people to understand the essence of Green Zone Philosophy and make it part of their lives, I share with them the following 12 Green Zone ideas.

GREEN ZONE IDEAS
1. *Though human beings can be their own worst enemies, Green Zone Philosophy helps them become their own best friends.*
As human beings, we all have a duality to our nature. We have a dark side and a bright side, a violent side and a peaceful side. At every turn in life and in every crisis, we make choices, some conscious, some unconscious. When we make unconscious and unhealthy choices, we become our worst enemies; but when we make conscious and healthy choices, we become our best friends. Green Zone Philosophy helps us stay in touch with our Green Zone so that we make wise and peaceful choices and become our best friends rather than our worst enemies.

2. *Green Zone is the other name for a peaceful mind.*

Those people who are in touch with their Green Zone feel connected with their peaceful centre, their inner voice, a reflection of their authentic self. Their mind becomes still like a lake that reflects the moon at night. They act according to their convictions and do not feel guilty as they have a clear conscience.

3. *Green Zone is our personal emotional thermometer.*

Becoming aware of our Emotional Zones is the first step towards changing our lives for the better. The more aware we are of the fluctuations, the better we are able to correct ourselves.

Studies in biofeedback have helped us understand that when people are made aware of their bodily functions — breathing, body temperature and heart beat patters — they developed more voluntary control over those functions which they previously believed were involuntary. The same theory applies to our emotional life. The more aware we are of the changes in our Emotional Zones, the more we are able to live in our peaceful Green Zone.

4. *In the Yellow Zone, wise people put their foot on the brake rather than on the accelerator.*

The metaphor for the emotional Green, Yellow and Red Zones was inspired by the traffic lights because there are some similarities between emotional rules and traffic rules. Many people who get into angry and bitter fights with their dear ones and lose control do not stop themselves in their Yellow Zone. They do not recognize that they have a choice to go forward and have an accident or stop and avoid a crisis. The more people become aware of their Yellow Zone, the more able they are to make a U-turn and come back to their peaceful Green Zone. In this way they do not risk landing in their painful Red Zone and losing control.

5. *Green Zone Communication takes place only when both parties are in their Green Zone.*

When people who are in their peaceful Green Zone are interacting with people who are in their angry Red Zone, they do not realize that rather than bringing them out of their Red Zone, it is more likely that they themselves would also fall into the Red Zone. People who are in their Red Zone act like drunks and throw angry bait that people who are in the Green Zone can easily swallow. It is wise for people who are in their Green Zone to wait until people who are in their Red Zone come back to their Green Zone so that both parties can engage in a fruitful discussion and a meaningful dialogue to share information and resolve conflicts peacefully and gracefully.

6. It is hard for people to stay in their Green Zone if they are part of a Yellow or Red Zone System, as systems are often emotionally stronger than individuals.

It is not uncommon for peaceful Green Zone people to feel distressed if they are living with stressful families or working in toxic work environments. Sooner or later such environments pull people into their negative vortex. If people have to live and work in such environments they need to create an Emotional Raincoat to decrease the negative effects. If possible it would be healthier to leave those environments and become part of peaceful Green Zone families and work systems.

7. Discovering one's special gift is a significant step towards creating a peaceful Green Zone Lifestyle.

Life has given all of us a special gift. Some discover it sooner than others. The Green Zone Philosophy encourages people to have a Green Zone Hour everyday to do what they love to do. Such a process can start as a hobby and then progress into a passion and a dream. By sharing one's special gift one can also create a circle of friends, a Green Zone Family of the Heart. In these Green Zone relationships people bring out the best in each other.

8. *In Green Zone Families, every person's special gift is acknowledged and cherished.*

Those people who grow up in neglectful Yellow Zone or abusive Red Zone families suffer for a long time. Fortunate are those people who grow up in nurturing and loving Green Zone families because in such families every person's special gift is acknowledged and cherished.

9. *Children need Green Zone families, schools and communities to become peaceful Green Zone adults.*

It is our collective responsibility to make sure that all children that come into this world receive the love and care they need in their families, schools and communities to become peaceful Green Zone adults. It is part of folk wisdom that we need "a whole village to raise a child". Children are our precious future. We need to take special care of them.

10. *Serving humanity helps people to discover their Green Zone.*

One does not need a Masters or a PhD in a caring profession to make a positive impact; all one needs is a caring mind and a compassionate heart.

11. *Green Zone People are motivated by love and peace rather than hate, violence and war.*

When we look around us, we find that hate is becoming a powerful motivator. There are some leaders of social groups, religious organizations and political institutions who are fighting political and economic wars with violence and are rationalizing their hate by saying that they are promoting peace and social justice, democracy and human rights. They want to promote peace by embracing violence. How sad! In the contemporary world we need more Green Zone people who are motivated by genuine love and peace.

12. *When Green Zone People become leaders, they inspire others to create Green Zone communities.*
When Green Zone People become leaders of social groups, religious organizations or political institutions, they inspire others. In the contemporary world we need more Green Zone leaders to take humanity to the next stage of human evolution.

The Happy, Healthy and Peaceful GREENZONE Living 7 Step Program

STEP ONE: Becoming aware of your Emotional Zones, either Green, Yellow, or Red.

STEP TWO: Recognizing changes in your Emotional Zones.

   Identify three things that push you to the Yellow and Red Zones.

STEP THREE: Recovering from the Yellow and Red Zones.

   Identify three things you can do to get back to your Green Zone.

STEP FOUR: Restraining from going into the Yellow and Red Zones.

   Identify three things you can do to stay in your Green Zone.

STEP FIVE: Creating Green Zone Relationships.

Dr. K. Sohail/Dr. Rizwan Ali

Make a list of all significant relationships and decide what Zone they are in and how you will deal with the Yellow and Red Zones relationships.

STEP SIX: Creating Green Zone Systems.

Identify the Zones of your Family, Work and Social Systems.

STEP SEVEN: Creating Your Green Zone Lifestyle

Discover your Special Gift - Creating, Sharing and Serving.

Chapter Seven

MICHELLE'S GREEN ZONE STORY

Dear Dr. Sohail,

When I first came to see you, I had a lot of "Red Zone" things going on in my life. My work life was a huge mess. I had a lot of difficulty in my work relationships with colleagues and administration. Being a high school teacher, I also had to deal with difficult students and difficult parents on top of not getting along with my vice-principal and principal. I was also tired of being used by certain colleagues, expecting me to take on their work as well as my own. This stress at work caused tension at home between me and my husband. Our usual happy-go-lucky relationship was deteriorating quickly, and our marriage was full of insults, sarcasm, and hate. This took a toll on our children, and one son in particular, stuck in the middle with no way out, began venting his own feelings of anger by harming other children at school, swearing at his teachers, and threatening to kill himself. This son, who was only eleven at the time, made life difficult for his two brothers, and even more so for me. This strained relationship with my son led to a very verbally abusive relationship with my mother, who I never really got along with anyway. So now things with her were even worse than before. I dealt with these poor relationships by complaining and crying to the people who I did have good relationships with, which ended up putting strain and tension on those good relationships, causing them to become "Red" as well. I also liked to shop a lot to make myself feel better, which led to financial worries that I had to deal with too. Nothing was going right in my life when I first came to see you. However, very soon after reading your book, *The Art of Living in your Green Zone*, I began to feel as if there was some hope for me.

With the first step, becoming aware of my *Emotional Zones*, what I had to learn was which "color" I was feeling, whether "Red", "Yellow", or "Green". I learned quickly that Green is basically any feeling that is positive and makes you feel good. Feeling Yellow meant that I was getting frustrated, annoyed, and was on the verge of raising my voice and saying nasty, hurtful things to people. For me, Red meant that I was absolutely being abusive to people verbally, that I couldn't carry on a conversation without yelling, screaming, insulting, hurting, or taking cheap shots at people. It meant that I was completely pissed off or depressed, lonely, in despair, and not able to function in any way at all. Once I learned these colors of emotion, I was able to identify easily what color I was experiencing at any given time. In the beginning of our sessions, I was always feeling Yellow or Red, which to me was ok, because at least I was now conscious of what type of emotion I was experiencing. It also helped that you asked me to keep track of my emotional colors throughout the day in a diary.

The second step, *recognizing changes in my Emotional Zones*, was also easy for me to pick up on, as it was simple to figure out when I became Yellow or Red, what things pushed me into those colors, what, or who, made me feel Yellow, and when did Yellow change to Red. Certain things came to my mind right away. When I walked through the door after a long day of work, I was always bombarded with information from my husband or the kids needing something. Usually I'd be dealing with phone messages, signing agendas, reading notes, being asked when supper would be ready, and somebody wanting me to drive them somewhere, all before I put my bag down and took my coat off. It made me feel overwhelmed, frustrated, and angry when that happened; all Red Zone feelings.

In order to get out of the Yellow and Red Zones, I had to experience what it might be like to be in the Green Zone. So in the third step, *recovering from my Yellow and Red Zones*, I had to figure out what things made me feel Green— happy, excited, joyful, pleased, relaxed, and so on. And then I had to actually do those Green Zone activities. For example, I had told you that spending quiet time alone, doing something for myself would make me feel relaxed, calm, and energized. You then gave me homework — spend one hour every evening for a month by myself, doing something that made me feel good. At first, this seemed impossible. How would I be able to get a whole hour to myself with a husband who works evenings and three children at home who needed help with homework, uniforms washed, supper made, and fights to be broken up? Not to mention the marking and other work related stuff that had to be done for the next day. But I found a way to make time to be in my Green Zone. At first I wasn't able to do an entire hour, but I eventually got to that point. An hour a day in the Green Zone eventually led to an afternoon in the Green Zone, then a whole day, and then a whole week. After a few months, and with a few other strategies, I was able to spend two whole weeks in the Green Zone, feeling happy, comfortable, rested, able, strong, and confident. I was able to have positive interactions and conversations with people! It felt great being Green for that long! Once I knew how to get into my Green Zone, I needed ways to stay there.

The fourth step, *restraining from going to the Yellow and Red*, was challenging. It required me to deal with Yellow and Red Zone people and situations, while remaining in the Green. This was difficult, especially if the other people I was dealing with did not know about the colors of emotion. I had to think of things that would bring me back to the Green if I did slip into Yellow and Red with other people. One thing I came up with was that it would be ok to say to someone that I would get back to them at a later time. So, for example, if my colleague needed me to do them a favor that would require a lot of time, effort, and energy that I didn't want to invest, usually I would have become very upset, uncomfortable, I would have felt like I was being used and that this colleague was a lazy so-and-so who could go to you-know-where, because I had enough "favors" that I had to do for myself. But Step Four taught me that instead, I could say, "I'll think about it and get back to you later." By saying this, I bought myself time to calm down, think rationally, and come back to them in a more positive mood, with a confident answer that would state clearly what I was able, or not able, to do for them. Step Four was eventually a lot easier once I started telling the people in my life what the colors of emotion were and what they meant.

Step Five, *creating Green Zone relationships*, came with mixed reactions. In this step, I was to tell the people in my life about the Green, Yellow, and Red Zones. This would help to create Green Zone relationships between me and the important people in my life. It meant that I would have to tell them about my therapy and how I now communicated and thought about feelings. This was fine when it came to my family, because they knew I was seeing you and that I was trying something new. The terms "Red", "Yellow", and "Green" became the new language used in my home with my children, husband, brother, and parents. Whenever one of us was feeling a certain way, the colors would come up to describe that feeling. For example, when I become overwhelmed now when first walking into the house, I just tell the kids, that "Mommy's feeling a little Yellow right now, could you come back to me when my coat is off, and my bag is away? I'll be Green by then. Thanks". Quite often I'll also hear one of my kids say to another, "You're making me feel "Red" and I don't like it!" So, it's working at home. Creating color language at work was a little harder for me, and so I only made it known to one or two people who I trust, feel comfortable with, and who I knew would appreciate the concept and this has created Green Zone relationships with them as well. There are other people at work who I have not shared the color zones concept with, which led me to Step Six.

Step Six is all about creating *Green Zone systems with your family, your work, and within your community.* Some systems, as mentioned before, are easy to do this with, and others are not so easy. For those systems or people who I cannot create a Green Zone relationship with, either because I am not comfortable, or they are not willing, I try to remember to wear my Emotional

Raincoat. So for example, I do not get along well with my principal at work. But I also do not have to interact with him on a regular basis, so it is not a relationship I would consider making Green by telling him about the colors of emotion. Instead, every time I must interact with him, I walk into the potentially Red situation and/or conversation feeling Green and wearing an imaginary raincoat (or in this case, an imaginary suit of armor) that will "protect" me from any Red things he may say or do. This suit of armor acts as my shield against any Red attacks that may come my way. This allows me to hear what he is saying without becoming Red. It also allows me to respond to him in a Green manner and leave the situation still feeling Green, and not allow him to affect how I feel in a major way. Sometimes, it is hard to wear the suit of armor or raincoat, and even though you may walk in wearing it, it somehow is not the right size, and ends up coming off, exposing you to the Red environment, and getting you covered in Red feelings. When this happens, I deal with it by accepting it. There are times when I have gone into a situation feeling Green, and my suit of armor has not worked, and so I come out feeling Red. In this case, I accept that I have felt some negative feelings, or thought some negative thoughts, or even reacted in a negative way, but I do not stay negative. I try to drive through the Red Zone instead of parking in it and staying that way. I have had to do that many times. Drive through the Yellow and Red Zones, but always make a U-turn back to the Green Zone. I believe this is healthy. It becomes unhealthy when I park in Red and stay there overnight.

The seventh step is the final step to following your colors of emotion concept. The seventh step is one that I am still currently working on, and will probably work on for the rest of my life. It requires me to create a *Green Zone lifestyle*. It means I will try to live in the Green Zone for the rest of my life while trying to serve the world in a peaceful, Green Zone way. For me, it means that I will try to set an example for other people by living Green. It means interacting with others in a Green way, seeing the world in a Green way, and contributing to my family, my work, and my community in a Green way. This can be difficult because it requires a constant effort in the beginning to always be aware of living in the Green, but as time goes on, it seems to get easier and easier. I'm finding that the more I feel Green, the more I act Green, and so the more I live Green, which shows in everything I do.

When I first came to you for help, I was in a very Red place. It was so Red, it was almost black. The relationships in my life were crumbling, my work was falling apart, my finances were melting into a sea of debt, my mood was negative, my behavior was abusive, and my children were becoming what I had become:

desperate, lonely, depressed, and in despair. And within a very short amount of time, with your help, I was able to understand and work through my troubles in just seven little steps. For that, Dr. Sohail, I will never be able to repay you, except to promise you that I will carry on your concept of the Red, Yellow, and Green Zones for the rest of my life, passing it on to my students and my children, who will hopefully, one day, live Green too, making the world just a little more Green; and it's all because of you.

   With great thanks,   Michelle

Chapter Eight

CREATING A MEANINGFUL LIFE

In the last few years a number of people who struggled emotionally because of meaninglessness of their life, came to my clinic to consult me as a psychotherapist. They did not suffer from any mental illness. They were not psychotic or clinically depressed. Their main complaint was,

"My life is meaningless"

"I have no purpose in life"

"My life is not fulfilling".

They wanted me to help them in creating a meaningful life.

While I was working with these people in therapy, I prepared a questionnaire and sent it to my friends and colleagues to find out how they discovered their meaning in life. I thought reading those responses might help and inspire my patients to create their own unique meaning in life. My questionnaire included the following four questions.

1. *Do you believe LIFE has a meaning? If yes, what is it?*

2. *Does YOUR LIFE have meaning? If yes, what makes it meaningful?*
3. *Did you ever feel YOUR LIFE was meaningless? If yes, how did you make it meaningful?*
4. *Do you consider yourself a religious, spiritual or a secular person? What is your philosophy of life?*

I was pleasantly surprised by the enthusiastic responses. Those responses ranged from 5 lines to 5 paragraphs to 5 pages. Interestingly in the respondents there were more men than women and more secular than religious people. When I read all the responses, I realized that their answers could be divided into the following groups.

1. *MEANINGFUL PERSONAL DREAMS*

A number of respondents had personal goals, ambitions and dreams that made their life meaningful. As they followed their passions and dreams, their life took a positive turn and became more enjoyable. Some wanted to develop their fullest potential while others wanted to develop their artistic talents and create masterpieces.

One respondent said, "One must live one's life to the fullest…ensuring one is true to oneself first and foremost…"

One artist responded, "Until I have created my 'masterpiece' there will be a void, but perhaps that is the pursuit of many artists."

A writer stated, "I read books, I write books, which makes life very meaningful."

One respondent quoted George Eliot who said, "It is never too late to become what you might have been."

2. *MEANINGFUL RELATIONSHIPS*

There were a number of respondents who found meaning in their emotional bonds. For them their friends, sweethearts, spouses, colleagues and relatives enriched their lives. One mother said, "My children make my life meaningful…" For many, loving relationships were a source of meaning in their lives.

One respondent stated, "What makes life meaningful is the fact that I have a family, have children, grandchildren, friends, relatives…."

3. *MEANINGFUL SERVICE TO HUMANITY*

There were a large number of respondents who believed that serving other human beings made their life meaningful. Their altruistic behavior helped them rise above their selfish mindset and made them part of humanity. They felt they were part of creating a happy, healthy and peaceful world. One respondent said, "My life has meaning because I care about other human beings. I have been involved in human rights issues since I was a teenager and I have been trying to educate people about that. Another task that I have taken upon myself is to encourage people to adopt scientific thinking and I have been quite successful in that. Those endeavors make my life meaningful. They make me feel that I HAVE made a difference."

4. *MEANINGFUL CONNECTION WITH GOD AND RELIGION*

A small number of respondents felt that their special relationship with their God and religion provided meaning to their lives. One respondent who suffered from depression said that belief in God helped many depressed people to stay alive, otherwise those who felt desperate would have committed suicide. He stated, "...in case of depression, it is religion that gives you support and a light for living, otherwise there should have been much more suicides in the world than occur at present. Everyone gets depression at one time or another. Some overcome it without any help, some need psychiatric help. Religion, right or wrong provides a good psychiatric support to overcome depression and provides a meaning to life and urge to live." One female Muslim stated, "I have always felt the presence of ALLAH around me and that has always been meaningful to me."

Another male Muslim wrote," So I am a Muslim and believe in One God, the Creator and the concept of life after death and accountability of my actions in this existing life. And this assumption or faith has made my life meaningful."

DOES LIFE IN GENERAL HAVE MEANING?
In my interview, alongside asking people about their personal life, I also asked them whether life in general had a meaning. Most secular people believed life had no intrinsic meaning while spiritual and religious people believed life had an inherent meaning. Some seemed unsure. One woman said "Life has a meaning but I do not know what it is". Some believed it SHOULD have meaning, otherwise life would be meaningless and the idea of a meaningless life made them uncomfortable. One respondent stated, "Every life must have had a meaning, for if not, then the whole act of creation becomes meaningless…"

It was interesting for me to see how for some religious people a faith in God and religion and for spiritual people their spiritual ideals made their lives meaningful. One Muslim stated, "My life has a meaning to serve ALLAH and be able to connect people with ALLAH". On the other hand, secular people did not need God, religion or spiritual values to make their lives meaningful. For them their art, music, loving relationships and serving humanity were enough to lead an enjoyable, exciting and meaningful life. For some secular people their spirituality was more connected with humanity than divinity. One secular respondent said, "I am very spiritual and a secular humanist. The source of spirituality is love, knowledge and above all music."

Some secular people had a unique perspective to meaninglessness of life. One stated, "I find meaningfulness of life in its meaninglessness." Another non-religious person felt meaning was not important to enjoy life. He said, "...overall I find my life most satisfying— whether with or without meaning"

Some secular people believed that as human beings evolve and grow and develop rational and logical thinking, their need for God and organized religions will become less and less. One respondent stated, "God was created by humans for psychological and emotional reasons. As human courage and wisdom grows further, God will be buried in the caves he came from."

It was fascinating to see how secular people searched for meaning in life without religious and spiritual traditions. One quoted Bertrand Russell for defining a good life, "A good life is one, inspired by love and guided by knowledge." The other responded that he tried to make his life meaningful by, "enjoying various thrills of life that nature has gifted us, with the least amount of guilt and repentance. He added, "I am extraordinarily conscious of my cosmic ignorance and I strive to be compassionately ego-less, carefully fearless and ethically guilt-free."

SERVING HUMANITY

Amongst all the religious, spiritual and secular respondents, alongside their differences of opinion, they had a reasonable consensus on one aspect. Most of them agreed that serving humanity was a major source of making their lives meaningful as such activities connected them with other human beings in a meaningful way.

One respondent said, "…One of the major pleasures is to be of some help to other human beings…" Such behaviors decrease human suffering and increase quality of life. Serving humanity creates genuine bonds and friendships between people where they rise above religious, cultural, gender and ethnic differences and connect with common humanity. It seems as if by serving humanity human beings can strive to become fully human individually and collectively, rise to the next stage of human evolution, and become part of creating a loving, just and peaceful world. One of my favorite responses was, "My aim is to be the best person I can be and to strive to change the world for the better even in a small way."

When I was reviewing the responses I realized that some people had accepted the traditional meaning of life, the meaning offered to them by their families, communities, religions and cultures, while there were others who had rejected the traditional meaning but found their own meaning to their lives.

When I shared the responses with the people I was working in my clinic who were struggling with meaninglessness in their lives and finding it distressing, they found those answers quite helpful. It offered them hope and inspired them to discover their own unique meaning by:

...focusing on their personal talents and pursuing a hobby, a passion and a dream. They finally got in touch with the special gift life had offered them but they had been unaware of it

...developing new relationships and creating a circle of close friends, that I call *family of the heart* and

...doing some voluntary work to serve their communities.

I was pleased that my friends sent thoughtful answers to my questions and I felt honored that my patients gave me an opportunity to help them in creating meaningful lives. Helping them also gave meaning to my life as a humanist psychotherapist.

SECTION TWO:
ADVANCED PRINCIPLES OF PSYCHODYNAMIC ASSESSMENT AND FORMAULATION
BY
DR RIZWAN ALI

Chapter Nine

PATIENT SELECTION

Historically, psychiatric patients have been placed into two broad categories: neurotic and psychotic. This distinction determines whether our patients are suitable for *intensive* or *supportive* psychotherapy. Discussing this concept in his book *Severe Personality Disorders*, Otto Kernberg explains his concept of "Cycling of Anchoring Symptoms". This concept emphasizes that to determine whether patients are operating from a neurotic or psychotic frame of mind, they should be examined in three areas of psychological functioning:

- *identity integration*
- *defensive operations* and

- *reality testing.*

NEUROSES

In Kernberg's *cycle of anchoring symptoms,* patients enter the *cycle* with mild symptoms, like mild sadness, mild anxiety, sleep disturbance, etc., as their presenting problem. Patients may remain symptomatic without ever developing a full-blown disorder. The next stage is when characterological or personality disorders start to emerge. In these early stages of symptomatology, *identity* and *reality testing* remain intact. Self-representations and object-representations are sharply demarcated — which means that there is no confusion between self and others and an individual identity is clearly maintained. A person has a comprehensive conception of self and others (integrated identity).

Defenses utilized at this level of functioning are generally "high-level defense mechanisms", including *reaction formation, isolation, undoing, rationalization* and *intellectualization.*

Reality testing is intact and the capacity exists to evaluate self and others realistically and in depth, without any doubt or confusion.

BORDERLINE CONDITIONS

In this stage of symptomatology, identity starts to become diffused and less integrated. Distinction between the good self/bad self is projected onto others and reintegrated, causing relationships to become rocky, fragile and unpredictable. Expectations of other people become unrealistic. The person tends to test and retest people unnecessarily. Due to an absence of internal integration (holistic view of self or others) such individuals experience others (and self) as totally good or totally bad "versions". The failure to integrate these conflicting aspects of self or others results in a lacuna in their intra-psychic existence which is impossible to fill with reassurances, love or compassion. Interactions with such individuals can be plagued by confusion, frustration and disappointments.

Defense mechanisms operate at a lower level — *splitting, primitive idealization, projective identification, denial, omnipotence* and *devaluation* play a major role, making trust and maintaining a relationship almost impossible.

When psychic functioning continues to be stressed, soft psychotic symptoms start to appear, like paranoia and altered perception. Basic reality testing is maintained but these patients are literally at the borderline state — between neuroses and psychoses.

FUNCTIONAL PSYCHOSES

In this stage, self-representations and object-representations are poorly delimited. In some cases there is delusional identity. Delusions and hallucinations emerge as manifestations of an ever-weakening (or failure to obtain) capacity to distinguish between "self" and "other". Manic-depressive illnesses, schizophrenia and other psychotic disorders represent this stage of worsened symptomatology.

The merging of *self* and *object* results in *regression and projection, denial* and other immature defenses which play a major role in the manifestation of this state of mind.

Reality is altered in thoughts and perceptions. The capacity to stay within the bounds of reality is lost.

Medications and sometimes hospitalization are needed to help these patients, and dynamic psychotherapy is generally not possible at this stage. Once stability on medications is achieved and later when reality testing is regained, an attempt can be made to challenge the patient's mind for more interpretive and expressive work, but this requires much experience, care and due diligence.

ORGANIC BRAIN SYNDROMES

The last part of this cycle of anchoring symptoms, as described by Kernberg, is called *Organic Brain Syndrome*. These syndromes include Traumatic Brain Injury, metabolic encephalopathies and other causes of damage to the brain's structural and functional integrity. Identity, defenses and reality testing are so impaired that they do not allow for a meaningful psychodynamic intervention or efficacy. These derangements of brain and therefore mind functioning can be divided into acute and chronic states. Acute states are usually characterized by their sudden onset, with disturbances in attention, concentration and orientation, as we see in delirium. These may or may not be reversible. Chronic states as exemplified by dementia of various forms render individuals inappropriate for psychodynamic therapies.

Disorders of intelligence, now called *Intellectual Disability*, are the last stage in this cycle, where comprehension, decision making and other higher faculties of the brain are not fully or adequately developed.

INITIAL ASSESSMENT

The initial dynamic interview is aimed at assessing the patient's position in the above-described continuum. Dynamic therapy is possible only when major faculties of mental functioning are still intact. Therefore, the boundary between borderline states and psychotic states directs what treatments will ultimately benefit the patient at the time of entry into treatment. If impairment is so significant, due to either functional psychosis (the lowest level of psychic resiliency) or organic impairment, dynamic therapies are neither appropriate nor effective. Other beneficial therapies can still be offered to these patients including *supportive psychotherapy* and pharmacotherapy.

SUPPORTIVE PSYCHOTHERAPY

One should never underestimate the usefulness and value of supportive techniques in psychiatry. Supportive psychotherapy serves several functions. Dr. Howard Book highlighted the importance of supportive psychotherapy in his book *Brief Psychodynamic Psychotherapy*.   Dr. Book notes the following:

1. Therapeutic Framework: Bringing consistency and safety to treatment helps promote a therapeutic relationship. Scheduling the time, place and duration of sessions sets the boundary for the treatment which helps the patient appreciate a structure and feel safe.

2. Empathy: The capacity of the therapist to understand situations from the patient's perspective is a great tool in psychotherapy. Empathy is not just being nice to the patient or feeling sorry for him. Empathy is the ability to get into someone else's shoes and feel the pain of the other person from that person's perspective.

3. Maintaining Defenses: For patients with a fragile and weak ego, some of the vital defenses are a great asset. Maintaining those defenses is the most important task of the supportive psychotherapist.

4. Setting Limits: Patients are asked to control their impulsivity during the treatment. Cutting behavior and the use of alcohol and illicit drugs is discouraged. Expression of emotions is encouraged through words, but physical acting-out is

never allowed. This helps patients learn self-restraint and later self-control.

5. Highlighting Progress: Some patients are so negative in their approach that they cannot appreciate the gains and advances they have made in their lives. The therapist helps them realize their strengths and achievements. It is very important in supportive psychotherapy that patients gain this insight into the better side of their selves.

6. Staying In the Here and Now: Supportive therapy helps patients focus on their current issues rather than dwelling on the past which results in depression, or worrying about the future which causes anxiety. *Here and Now* brings a better and clearer perspective to life and the patient learns to live in the moment.

7. Showing Genuine Interest and Respect: If the therapist is bored, irritated and uninterested in his patient's story then no work is possible. Showing genuine interest in and respect for the patient are two very important tools in therapy. Some patients have not seen this in their entire lives, and finding someone really interested in them makes a huge difference in the way they start seeing themselves.

DYNAMIC PSYCHOTHERAPY

Selecting patients suitable for Dynamic Psychotherapy is an important aspect of predicting their response to treatment. It should be emphasized that there collective impression or constellation of attributes exists which makes a patient a suitable candidate for dynamic psychotherapy. If someone has one or two qualities and lacks the rest, he may not be amenable to this kind of work. A person may be very intelligent and accomplished; however, if he lacks the ability to tolerate frustration and is exhibiting poor impulse control, he may not endure the anxiety that dynamic therapy can frequently create. In his book *The Practice of Supportive Psychotherapy,* Dr. David Werman offers a detailed list of characteristics of the ideal patient for psychotherapy:

Ego Strength: Ego is the dynamic energy which defines us as an individual. Ego functions are numerous; everything that we feel or do is a function of our ego, including perception, locomotion, speech, memory, defenses, reality testing, self-observation (introspection), experience, appreciation of feelings, object relations, verbal ability and control of impulses. Judgement, cognition, the possession of sublimatory assets, and the tolerance of mental pain are all functions of ego. Therefore, everything listed hereafter is an ego function. In a nutshell, the basic assessment in initial interviews is of ego strengths and weaknesses.

1. **Reality Testing:** This is the most important test to differentiate patients with psychosis. Soft psychotic symptoms are common in patients with Borderline Personality Disorder but that does not make them unsuitable for dynamic therapy. Similarly, after effective treatment of psychosis with medications, the same person may benefit from more exploratory work.

2. **Impulse Control:** If a person is not capable of delaying his impulse to act physically and does not prefer to express himself verbally, he may not be suitable for intensive work. However, one should differentiate between primary and secondary impulse control problems. If poor impulse control is coming from a treatable psychiatric or general medical condition then a fair attempt should be made first to treat that condition and then re-evaluate the patient. One such condition is bipolar mania; the other is intoxication or withdrawal from the abuse of alcohol or other substances. Once treated, underneath all that noise may be

found a very different, quite workable human being.

3. **Psychological-Mindedness:** This may be understood as the collective impression of the person, after detailed and complete evaluation, based on all of the qualities listed in this chapter. Psychological-mindedness is defined in an article in the American Journal of Psychotherapy (1992) by J. A. Hall as, "reflectivity about psychological processes, relationships, and meanings, and is displayed by an individual to the extent that he or she displays both interest in and ability for such reflectivity, and across both affective and intellectual dimensions. Ability is contributed to and limited by interest, and intellectual psychological-mindedness is contributed to and limited by affective psychological-mindedness". There are a number of articles in the literature defining this capacity for self-examination, self-reflection, introspection and personal insight, as a most important predictor of insight-oriented/dynamic psychotherapy outcome.

4. **Intelligence:** A minimum adequate "average" intelligence is required for psychotherapy. After all, the treatment

requires comprehension, reflection and expression of complex emotions, and feeling and understanding of what is being said and what is happening in the session. Patients with limited intelligence and significant impairment in their cognitive functioning may benefit from supportive psychotherapy instead of dynamic work. Sometimes "too much" intelligence can be a hindrance, as well. When patients come in with an announcement that they have read "all of Freud, Jung and Kernberg", and declare that they are smarter than the therapist, it becomes very challenging even for experienced therapists to break through that defense of intellectualization and work around it to deal with the true feelings underneath. It does not mean that intelligence is always an obstacle; it can be very beneficial if it serves the individual in his best interest and if it allows him to focus his attention in the right direction.

5. **Age:** Of course, very young children may need a special kind of therapy called "play therapy" and very elderly people with obvious cognitive deficits and memory problems may not be suitable for intensive dynamic work. Other than that, age need not include or exclude anyone for therapy.

Issues in life change according to age and focus in therapy may change accordingly. For example, for teenagers identity, independence and individuality may be the most important topics, while for older patients relationships, work and the meaning of life may be the focus of therapy. By taking into account all of these stage-of-life contents, the experienced therapist is able to focus on the process and help his patients.

6. **Verbal Ability:** Another name for dynamic therapy is expressive or "talk therapy"; therefore, reasonable verbal skill is a pre-requisite for this type of treatment. Chatty or eloquent patients may cause distraction from the actual work. Similarly, silence may be useful for the session, if utilized appropriately, at the right place and for the right duration of time. If silence is due to resistance, that should be explored; but if paucity of speech is interfering with the progress, then other types of therapy should be considered.

7. **Success in School or Work:** Success as measured in effective performance at work or school is an indicator of ego strength in relative, rather than absolute terms. Doing well at work with frequent promotions or

achieving good grades at school does not always mean that the person is psychological-minded, has the required insight into his problems, and is willing to explore and work on them. Similarly, failures can be due to unfortunate circumstances and do not always indicate that the person has issues with relationships or has a developmental arrest. Individual evaluation, rather than making a hasty decision based on one or two qualities, is therefore very important.

8. **Introspection:** A unique trait which allows someone "to step outside of himself' and view his behavior dispassionately and with some degree of objectivity" is perhaps the most important factor in determining whether the patient is suitable for dynamic psychotherapy (Dr. David Werman). Without this trait, the patient tends to blame others and the environment for his troubles and is not suitable for insight-oriented/intensive psychotherapy. One needs to be optimally curious about his behavior, feelings and thought processes to be able to get engaged in this type of therapy. If the patient keeps blaming their fate, their birth order, their race or the gods for all of his shortcomings

and misfortunes, then he may be more suitable for supportive psychotherapy.

9. **Ability to Sublimate:** A more creative and mature way of discharging sexual and aggressive energies is to divert these energies towards productive and useful activities beneficial to other human beings. This characteristic is indicative of a person's healthy self-esteem and his capacity to relate with others in a meaningful manner with mutual respect and gain.

10. **Tolerance of Suffering:** Emotional tension may run high when old patterns are challenged and new skills are learned. One of the most important goals of dynamic psychotherapy is to replace defective defenses with healthy and mature ones. The patient may regress if he is unable to tolerate this mental tension and frustration, and that may result in severe anxiety, guilt and depression. To be able to participate in this self-exploratory journey one needs some of this "mental muscle" to be able to bear the tension necessary for this kind of work.

11. **Relationships with Others:** The most important gateway to one's inner world is

through the examination of the quality of one's relationships. From birth to the present time, our relationships are the cardinal factor which defines us. Rocky, unstable, volatile relationships throughout one's life are indicative of poor psychological organization; such individuals may not tolerate the frustration required of dynamic therapy and may have difficulty trusting the therapist. On the other hand, mature, lasting and enriching relationships indicate that the person is suitable for intensive therapy.

Dynamic psychotherapy is based on the development of transference and the use of that transference in a therapeutic manner. People who lack this ability to relate to others in a meaningful way with emotional investment are not capable of developing transference towards a therapist. They may be more suited for supportive psychotherapy where transference is not needed for treatment. Some patients may appear on the surface to have very smooth and close relationships, but with deeper clarification it becomes evident that their motives are very self-centered and their intentions are to manipulate others for their benefit. We see those characteristics in people with narcissistic and antisocial personalities. Similarly, those who appear isolative should not be discarded for dynamic work because there may be depth and quality in their few but long and enduring relationships.

The presence of healthy and loving relationships with friends, spouses, siblings and co-workers is an important indicator of the good quality of a person's object relations and is extremely important in dynamic psychotherapy.

12. **Ego Defenses:** To protect the self from suffering, pain and conflict, defense mechanisms are active from early childhood. With a loving and caring upbringing one develops mature and healthy defenses, with several to choose from. When someone has only one or two of these numerous defenses, he will be very guarded and will be very reluctant to lose any one of them. Fear of losing defenses leaves a person with high vulnerability and great deal of apprehension which interferes with trust and ultimately with exploratory work. The quality of defenses is also very important; if someone relies on *acting out* rather than *sublimation* to deal with a certain stress, he may not be able to handle the suffering

inherent in dynamic therapy. *Denial, projection* and *splitting* are few more examples of immature defenses which will counter and resist any progress made in intensive therapy.

13. **Trust:** It is obvious that if the patient is suspicious and paranoid during the process of therapy, he will remain guarded throughout the treatment. Some amount of basic trust is required to start the process. Embarking on a journey with a stranger to explore one's feelings and go to the deeper recesses of the underwater caves of one's unconscious requires a tremendous amount of courage and trust. If someone is resistant and guarded, he should be referred to supportive psychotherapy.

14. **Motivation:** Alongside will, strong motivation is of utmost importance in dynamic therapy. Many patients may have the desire to change and improve but how motivated they are and how much they are willing to sacrifice is ultimately going to make the difference. Everyone's life is busy, and if motivation is lacking, excuses are numerous. Motivation is the energy that will encourage the patient to come to his appointments on time and make other adjustments in his life to be able to pay for

his therapy. This motivation will make the person work hard to accomplish the results. Without motivation, treatment becomes passive and is destined to fail.

15. **Role of Diagnosis:** Except for patients with structural brain damage and limited intellectual abilities, everyone else should be considered and assessed for dynamic psychotherapy. If all of the above qualities are considered, diagnosis itself plays a minor role in the selection of a patient for intensive work. Altered mental status or a psychotic and delusional state of mind makes it impossible to do much work; but once the storm subsides and symptoms are treated with medications and other therapies, the patient should be evaluated again for his psychological strengths and weaknesses. Substance abuse is one example: a patient may drink heavily to deal with his grief, but once the grief is processed and dealt with, he may never abuse alcohol again. Similarly, if a patient is currently manic, after the effective treatment of his mania he may be quite suitable for intensive work.

SUMMARY

In summary, the evaluation of a patient's suitability for psychodynamic therapy rests with the treating therapist, based on all of the qualities discussed above. Referrals made by other clinicians for psychodynamic therapy may not always be well-informed and each case requires scrutiny by the treating clinician. Though a comprehensive evaluation will determine the suitability of a candidate for dynamic therapy, a therapeutic compatibility between clinician and patient may not be optimal. A clash of personality styles that cannot be reconciled early in therapy may require a referral to another therapist. Also important is the therapist's degree of comfort and years of experience. With years of practice, a therapist may be able to deal with the patient's inner conflicts (transferences) and be aware of his or her own inner conflicts (counter-transferences) which may otherwise slow down the progress of treatment.

There are several types of dynamic psychotherapies, much as there are several dialects of a particular language. The therapist may be versed in one or two and the patient might respond optimally to yet a third. For example, if a therapist is trained in *transactional therapy* but the patient is more suitable for *existential therapy*, then a referral to an expert in that area may be the best. For trainees and beginners, exposure to multiple therapeutic options should be encouraged — they can then choose the types of therapy which interest them and suit their individual personalities.

Selecting a patient for the appropriate type of psychotherapy for a patient is an important aspect of psychiatric training. It should hold the same value as selecting the appropriate medication, dose, duration and setting of pharmacologic and other somatic treatments. The practice of this discipline of medicine is an art which improves with training, supervision and experience.

Chapter Ten

HISTORY AND PHYSICAL EXAMINATION

Any psychodynamic formulation is preceded by a detailed history and physical examination. Clinicians are trained from the beginning in the art of history taking. Comprehensive history taking requires a trusting relationship between the patient and the clinician and also a comfortable and private setting in which the patient feels relaxed and calm enough to open up. The initial interview begins at the referral when the clinician starts gathering basic data about the patient.

IDENTIFYING DATA

The patient's name, age, sex, race, marital status, occupation, education and living situation contribute information that tells a lot about patient's current situation and psychological make-up. Whether the patient is self-referred, or referred by a family member or other provider, also sheds important light on the patient's motivation and insight. The reason for referral is extremely important when thinking about expectations and dispositions. If a patient is referred for therapy with acute psychosis or agitated and manic symptoms, it may be appropriate to start gathering more information regarding his history of compliance with medications, and if appropriate a consult with a psychiatrist or the patient's primary care physician should be made prior to giving the patient an appointment. Unless the patient is stable enough to sit for an hour or two and is able to tolerate the stress of an interview with the clinician, there is no point in starting to evaluate him for psychotherapy.

CHIEF COMPLAINT

This is the presenting problem with which a patient comes to the clinician's office to seek help. This opening statement by the patient reveals his main source of distress. For example, "I am anxious" tells the clinician immediately that he is dealing with an anxious patient and may have to adjust his pace accordingly and say a few words of comfort before proceeding with the tough questions. Sometimes the patient starts the session by saying. "I am okay". This is not enough to call it a chief complaint. Further exploration is needed by asking, 'So what brought you to the clinic?" or, "how may I help you?"

HISTORY OF PRESENT ILLNESS

This is the story which the patient tells about his struggles. From the onset of symptoms until the present, a detailed and comprehensive history is the main tool which psychiatrists and psychologists rely on to help them with differential diagnoses and a treatment plan. Here expertise plays a major role. With experience the clinician gets better at gathering all necessary information about the positive and negative symptoms related to a patient's presenting problem in a timely manner. It includes all previous treatments and hospitalizations and their good or bad results. What helped and what did not help? Each syndrome - depression, anxiety or schizophrenia - needs to be explored in detail so that nothing is overlooked or unattended. A history of suicide attempts is particularly important and should be explored with special emphasis on recent ideas, intent and means. Homicidal ideas and plans are equally important to be ruled out and responses should be carefully documented.

LEGAL HISTORY

History of trouble with the law, imprisonment or jail time tells the clinician about patients' difficulties dealing with rules and laws and indicates a high degree of impulsivity and possible recklessness. If the patient is on probation or if the treatment is mandated by the court, this will help the clinician gauge the motivation in the patient himself. Sometimes outside forces compel the person to come for treatment before he is ready for a change. This can cause a major hindrance to recovery and resistance to improvement. On the other hand, sometimes this legal trouble becomes an eye-opener and a life-changer for the person. Therefore the clinician should be cognizant of the impact of legal issues in the patient's life.

HISTORY OF SUBSTANCE ABUSE

A detailed history of substance abuse is very important for obvious reasons. Some patients tend to minimize their use of alcohol, cigarettes or illicit drugs. Some believe that cannabis is helpful and relaxing and should not be classified as an illicit drug. Others believe that beer is not alcohol but just a recreational drink. Without getting into a philosophical or political discussion, the clinician needs to document the facts. Also important is whether the patient has received treatment for substance abuse and whether or not it was helpful.

MEDICAL AND SURGICAL HISTORY

Several psychiatric conditions may have a medical cause or may be a side effect of a medication. Stimulants prescribed to treat sleep disorders and ADHD may cause anxiety. Steroids and beta blockers are known to cause depression.

Thyroid conditions may result in psychiatric manifestations. A complete history of all medical problems and surgical procedures along with the list of current medications is a must at the time of initial intake.

FAMILY HISTORY

Both medical and psychiatric conditions have genetic and familial predispositions. It is important to know if a family member has attempted or committed suicide or had a history of depression or other psychiatric conditions. Sometimes it is useful to know which medication helped other family members because this might be the best choice in the patient as well.

SOCIAL AND DEVELOPMENTAL HISTORY

An elaborate social history is of paramount importance to a good psychodynamic formulation. Every effort should be made to collect the information on a timeline.

1.   Childhood and Teenage years: Birth order, significant events and traumas, siblings, and overall environment in the house where the person grew up shapes the person's psychological make-up for the rest of his life. Childhood traits and parental traits determine the course of mental attitude and growth in general. School

performance and the ability to adapt and make friends show an ability to tolerate stress and plasticity of mind. Significant relationships with peers and sexual and romantic relationships at an early age are extremely important indicators of the quality of future relationships.

2. Adulthood: The circumstances around moving out of the home and pursuits of education and employment indicate the degree of emotional stability. Military experience and particularly combat exposure changes life forever. Witnessing atrocities and participating in some of them, is a heavy burden to carry for most soldiers in civilian life. Duration, quality and depth of romantic, sexual and intimate relationships indicate a person's degree of trust and ability to share and give. Close friends and a support network, including involvement in altruistic activities, all indicate a healthy and resilient personality. Children and the patient's relationship with them are also very important. Involvement in hobbies, recreation and leisure activities tells if the person has healthy self-esteem and is able to relax, recoup, rejuvenate, and bounce back after a crisis. Retirement can be a testing time for some and can be a gift for others. How one handles a change in life is a great indicator of how satisfied that person is with the life he has lived so far.

MENTAL STATUS EXAMINATION

A comprehensive and detailed mental status examination is the best clinical tool for psychiatrists and psychologists. This is an objective determination of presence or absence of symptoms with tests for memory and other cognitive abilities including orientation, concentration and attention span. Mood, affect, perceptual and thought abnormalities, if any, are also documented in a succinct and standardized fashion. As are comments about suicidal/homicidal ideas or plans. In the end, judgement, insight and general knowledge are assessed and documented.

WORKING DIAGNOSES

All the information which has been gathered so far, along with the mental status examination, should point towards one or two working diagnoses.

Case Example
By Dr. Tenzing Yangchen – third year psychiatry resident (2015-16)

Psychodynamic Case Presentation
History and Physical
Identification Data

Mrs. C is a 40 year old Caucasian married female who has a past psychiatric history of Bipolar Disorder, Borderline Personality Disorder, Post-

Traumatic Stress Disorder (PTSD), and remote history of Alcohol Dependence. She was last seen by Dr. S in June last year.

Chief Complaint:
"I have PTSD".

<u>History of Present Illness</u>
Patient presents for her appointments on time. She was voluntarily readmitted to inpatient psychiatry in June last year after her follow-up appointment with Dr. S during which she endorsed a continued and worsening depressed mood, suicidal ideation, and poor sleep, following her request to be prematurely discharged in late May, when she presented with passive homicidal ideation in the context of an altercation with a biker, exacerbating her PTSD.

Over the weeks prior to her readmission, she had been to several outpatient appointments and testing, where she felt overwhelmed and misunderstood as she felt that her outpatient providers were beginning to doubt her diagnosis. During the admission, the dose of her bedtime Diazepam was increased to 10 mg to help with her anxiety and sleep, Trazodone was discontinued, and Mirtazapine was added to improve sleep and mood. She was continued on all other outpatient medications. She tolerated the changes and was discharged with stable mood and cessation of suicidal ideation.

Patient reports that she is working to rebuild her relationships with her therapy providers. She reports fair sleep, normal appetite, and stable mood *since her discharge from the hospital. She is tolerating her medications, which are dispensed by her husband due to her history of multiple overdoses in the past. She denied any auditory or visual hallucinations, suicidal or homicidal ideas, or labile mood.*

<u>*Past Psychiatric History*</u>
History of Bipolar Disorder, Depression with Psychotic Features, Borderline Personality Disorder, history of Multiple Substance Abuse, history of Alcohol Dependence, history of Schizoaffective Disorder, history of Factitious Disorder, history of Eating Disorder (Bulimia), and PTSD.

Patient reports that she was in therapy from age 8 till 15. She does not recall the reason for it but states that her mother told her it was to help her and her family.

She has attempted suicide via overdose of Tylenol about 9 times. She reports being in the ICU a few times. She has been psychiatrically hospitalized multiple times with the first admission 12 years ago after overdosing on Tylenol, followed by the Outpatient Mental Health Clinic thereafter with multiple readmissions and overdoses. Records show that the patient had a sub-therapeutic relationship with providers as she was noted to embellish her stories at times, which led to her receiving a diagnosis of Factitious Disorder.

She moved to Virginia around 2012 and has had 5 inpatient admissions since, with the last three in 2015. She usually presents with depression, anxiety and suicidal ideation. She was being followed by Dr. S and is currently in Dialectal Behavioral Therapy and Post-Traumatic Stress Disorder treatment groups.

Past medication trials include Aripiprazole, Citalopram, Diazepam, Haloperidol, Lamotrigine, Lithium, Prazosin, Quetiapine, Ramelteon, Trazodone, Topamax, Effexor, Ambien, Carbamazepine, Amitriptyline, Depakote, Clonazepam, Lorazepam, Sertraline, Hydroxyzine, Risperdal, Ziprasidone, Temazepam, Mirtazapine.

Past Medical/Surgical History

Migraine Headaches, Celiac Disease, Iron Deficiency Anemia, Primary Insomnia, history of Cervical Dysplasia, Obesity.

Total abdominal hysterectomy with bilateral salpingo-oophorectomy with history of Pelvic Inflammatory Disease (PID) and Endometriosis.

Allergies
Aspirin, latex, fish, turkey, influenza vaccine

Current Medications
Escitalopram 20 mg PO daily
Lamotrigine 100 mg PO BID
Lithium 300 mg PO QAM and 600 mg QPM
Mirtazapine 7.5 mg PO QHS
Prazosin 5 mg PO QHS
Ramelteon 8 mg PO QHS
Diazepam 5 mg PO BID and 10 mg QHS

Family History

Mother: Bipolar-depression per records. Per patient she does not know of any actual diagnosis or treatment. No history of suicide attempts in the family.

Social History
Childhood

Patient was born at 6.5 lbs., 12.5 inches long, in Ohio, into an affluent, family. She never knew her father as her mother was reported to have been divorced while her mother was 2 months pregnant. She has a sister, who is 8 years older. She recalls having had a poor relationship with her mother, sister and maternal grandmother.

Her grandmother thought she was evil and she and her older sister, blamed her for her mother's divorce. She does not recall ever being praised for anything or loved by her mother, which was not true of her relationship with her older sister. She was never breastfed and recalls being tiny. She states that she was always made fun of at school for being tiny and short. She lived in her mother's home with her nanny and helpers as her mother was never home.

She was essentially raised by her maternal grandfather, who was the only person who loved and protected her. She recalls only good memories of him and how he intentionally did things in church to annoy her mother, such as keeping her on his lap when she was supposed to be kneeling. She states that she was baptized by her grandfather and not her mother which was rare in their church. She was deeply affected by his demise when she was age 9 and recalls being inconsolable at the funeral.

Prior to his death, she was informed by him that he had prevented her mother from aborting her. He also told her how her mother as well as her grandmother and older sister refused to hold her after birth. It was hinted to her that her father was not her biological father but she did not comprehend it then.

She states that she was a trouble maker along with her one and only best friend "Liz", whom she befriended around age 3 or 4. They have continued and remain friends to date. They were dubbed the "terrible two" by their neighbors and they were assumed to be the culprits for any trouble caused in the neighborhood. For example, they would sneak out together, throw raw eggs at a neighbor's house, break curfews, skip school, and get into fights at school. She reports that this would make her mother very angry. She recalls always fighting with her mother and being compared to her sister in everything, especially academics. She has mentioned in the past records that her mother paid attention to her only when she misbehaved.

She reports that she was more into art and crafts in school than academics, and that she was particularly poor at math. She started cheerleading in kindergarten and continued into high school. She reports being active in cheerleading and playing the trumpet in a marching band. She reports having enjoyed being a cheerleader and the attention she received from it. She recalls having been asked to a junior prom when she was a freshman by a junior football player.

Becoming a Psychotherapist

She started seeing a psychotherapist at age 8 and states that she was raped by him twice. She became pregnant by him at 10, with a girl, whom she was made to give up in a closed adoption. She recalls holding her baby for a few minutes and being told that the adopting parents' name would be listed on her birth certificate. She states that her mother did not believe her when she reported the rape and instead suspected that she had gotten herself pregnant by her male friend. She reports that the therapist told her that he was her surrogate father after the demise of her grandfather, which she did not appreciate.

She reports attending school and continuing with cheerleading during the pregnancy, although she was looked down upon.

She reports that at 13 she ran away from home with money she had gotten by forging her mother's signature and recalls having withdrawn it from her trust left to her by her grandfather, which was overseen by her mother. She was found by police and dropped off at a group home where she remained for 3 months.

Per record review, the patient is noted to have been sexually abused by her uncle and a church priest/counselor in the past, which she did not mention. She states that her mother never believed that she was raped and blamed her male friends, whom she denied having any romantic/sexual relations with.

During her freshman and sophomore years in high school, the patient tried multiple substances such as heroin, speed, ecstasy, cocaine, methamphetamines, angel dust etc. She denies that she stuck with any one *drug. She completed sophomore year and dropped out of high school when she turned 16.*

Adulthood

She asked to be an emancipated minor at age sixteen and her mother willingly gave her up. She got her General Educational Development (GED) the next day and later joined the military. She was introduced to alcohol in the military as she was an emancipated minor and legally allowed to drink on the base. She admits that she was an alcoholic and drank heavily. She entered a 6-month inpatient rehab program while in-service and another 6-month program that was court mandated. She remained on probation for a year and has been sober for the past 12 years.

Her first marriage was at age 17 to a police officer who was 4 years older. She states that her mother was not supportive and made limited financial contributions towards the ceremony. She recalls that her mother did not dress up for the occasion, unlike her sister's marriage, when she had a dress especially made for her. The marriage lasted for about 14 months as they were often apart due to their work. She was also physically abused by her husband which led to the divorce.

She was honorably discharged from the military 15 years ago. In hindsight, she regrets having left the military as she felt that the structure was good for her and she was appreciated for the work that she did.

She had continued her education in the military and completed her bachelor's in business management. Soon after her discharge from the military, she started to work as a stock broker. She reports being responsible for accounts worth millions of dollars, but could not handle the stress and gave up the job. She started seeing a psychiatrist and reports she had her first manic episode at age 25. She has been on disability since early 2000 and currently is 100% disabled.

She remarried in 2000, to another man who was a gentleman during their courtship. She was unaware of his drug abuse until their honeymoon, when he presented her with several drugs, which she refused to take. He started to physically abuse her in the months following the marriage and she remained in it for only about a year, when she decided to leave and seek help at a domestic abuse shelter. They helped her file for divorce, etc.

Later, she met her current husband who is 25 years older than her. They had been friends for a long time before their marriage. He is very supportive of her and has been with her through her multiple hospitalizations and overdoses. They have been married for 8 years now and he is her best friend. She notes that she sees some of her grandfather in him. They have no children together but she is very close to his children and his grandchildren.

Because of her poor relationship with her family and their judgmental and emotionally abusive attitude towards her, which has been a constant variable in her multiple suicide attempts and hospitalizations, her husband decided to remove her from the toxic environment. She had one suicide attempt which was secondary to an email from her mother severing her ties with her. Patient states that she has not been in communication with her family for several years.

She has since been following up with an outpatient clinic in Virginia. She recently received her alleged father's death certificate and has concluded that he was not her biological father. She compared it to her birth certificate and found several inconsistencies.

Denied any legal history.

Mental Status Exam

Appearance: 40 year old, obese female, who appears stated age, dressed appropriately with good hygiene and grooming.

Attitude: calm and co-operative with good eye contact.

Behavior: No unusual movements or psychomotor changes.

Speech: Normal in volume, rate and tone without pressure.

Mood: Good.

Affect: Reactive and euthymic.

Thought form/ process: liner, logical and goal directed. No flight of ideas.

Thought content: No suicidal/homicidal ideation, intent or plan.

Perceptions: No hallucinations or delusions noted during the interview.

Orientation: Alert, awake and Oriented to time, place and person.

Memory/Concentration: Grossly intact.

Insight/judgment: Intact.

Working Diagnoses

Bipolar Disorder MRE depressed – stable on medications.

Borderline Personality Disorder

PTSD - stable

Alcohol Use Disorder in sustained remission

Opioid Use Disorder in sustained remission

Celiac Disease

Obesity

Interventions

No new medication changes since discharge. She is tolerating her medications and compliant with them.

Discussed the adverse effects of being on benzodiazepine, and polypharmacy in general.

Already in Dialectical Behavioral Therapy and PTSD groups.

Battery of psychological testing done recently including MMSE (22/30), WAIS-IV, WRAT4, PAI, SCID I, Vineland adaptive behavior scale, TOMM, SIMS.

Dr. K. Sohail/Dr. Rizwan Ali

Chapter Eleven

PSYCHODYNAMIC FORMULATION

Psychodynamic formulation starts after a working diagnosis is established in the light of a comprehensive and detailed history, physical and mental status examination. A psychodynamic interview is different than the medical interview and focuses on the strengths and weaknesses of the ego and operating defense mechanisms. After a comprehensive dynamic interview for one or two sessions (each one lasting for 1-2 hours) the formulation is prepared.

Generally there are three areas which are covered in a dynamic formulation:

1. RELATED FACTORS:

Factors contributing or leading to the current distress are listed here. There may be multiple factors worth mentioning in one case, whereas there may be only a few identifiable factors causing the problem in another. These factors include:

A.   Predisposing Factors: Factors that are there to begin with.

a.   Inherited/genetic: Family   history   of mental illness.

b.   Biological/organic: Traumatic brain injury, medical problems, etc., contributing to psychiatric symptoms.

B.   Precipitating Factors: Major event or events contributing to current symptoms like *the straw that broke the camel's back*. For example, loss of a loved one, losing a job or major change in one's health status with a diagnosis of some serious medical problem like cancer or fracture.

C.   Perpetuating Factors: Factors which keep symptoms alive, like alcoholism or ongoing trauma.

D.   Protective   Factors: Strengths   like education,   family   support,   willingness   to participate in treatment, compliance and positive relationships with family, friends and therapists.

      2.   *DYNAMIC ASSESSMENT:* This is the main part of the dynamic formulation. It requires knowledge and expertise to assess a patient based on the basic psychodynamic principles and contemporary theories of the mind. To help the clinician cover other areas and

modalities of treatments and come up with a more holistic view of the patient, it is advised that this section of the formulation should start with the observable conflicts and defense mechanisms.

Worldwide, the consensus is to cover the formulation from three different angles/theories/perspectives: *Ego Psychology, Object-Relations Theory and Self-Psychology.*

A. EGO PSYCHOLOGY:

Three areas are explored under this category:

1. STRUCTURAL MODEL: Freud introduced the "structural model" in the early 1900s. This model describes mental energies in three distinct forms. Id, Super-ego and Ego are all interconnected and dynamic in nature.

a. **Id** (Latin for "it"), is primarily unconscious, and contains basic human instinctual drives. Sleep, appetite, sex and self-preservation all fall under this part of our mind. All libidinal energies, either aggressive or sexual, are expressed through this channel. We are born with these instincts.

b. **Super-ego,** on the other hand, determines our value system, morals and ethics, and is manifested in restraints and delays of the libidinal instincts derived from the Id. We learn these values from our society, parents, teachers, churches, schools and legal system.

c.   **Ego** is the modulating part of our mind. Here the negotiation takes place. Part of the Ego is unconscious and that is where repression and defense mechanisms operate. The Ego has multiple functions including attention and memory; but the most important function is to negotiate between the Id and the Super-ego and come up with the best compromise possible without causing distress or anxiety. Any unresolved conflict between the opposite polar tensions of the Id and the Super-ego creates a tension in the Ego which manifests itself as restlessness and anxiety. Therapy is geared towards resolving that tension after processing the conflict.

A psychodynamic formulation from an Ego Psychology perspective attempts to understand the strengths and weaknesses of all of these three mental parts in an individual. During the interview, paying attention to the push and pull of the Id and the Super-ego and evaluating the capacity of the Ego to resolve these conflicts and find a balance (psychic homeostasis) is what is formulated under this heading.

2.   STAGES   OF   PSYCHOSEXUAL DEVELOPMENT: Another area that is emphasized under the Ego Psychology part of the formulation is the "Stages of Psychosexual Development". In the first five years of life, most of the blueprint is laid out for one's future psychodynamic growth, development of personality and emotional matrix.

a.   *Oral stage*: This is the stage of dependency from birth till 18 months of age. This is the time of life when the child learns to trust others. With lack of locomotion, he is totally dependent on his caretaker to feed, clean, hold him, and take care of his other needs. Love is unconditional and gradually becomes reciprocal.

b.   *Anal stage*: In this stage (18 months to 3 years of age) the child starts to walk and starts to claim his so-called independence. Sphincters start to operate according to one's will and desire. Toilet training becomes the hallmark of this stage and it marks the stage of autonomy. The child learns to realize that he is a separate individual and has his own existence. If navigated properly, several forms of identities start to emerge from the person which ultimately take shape in the next stage. He is able to get a cohesive sense of self with a warm assurance from his caretakers and the world in general.

c.   *Phallic stage*: This is the stage from age 3 till 5. This is the stage when the child learns to identify gender differences. Along with the realization of gender differences, conflicts like Oedipus and Electra emerge and resolve. This resolution determines how comfortable one is with his/her own self and identities, and also how comfortable he/she is dealing with and relating to other people in the future.

A clear understanding of "arrest" versus "regression" at a certain stage of development is very important in formulating a case. If the individual has never been able to move forward in a successful manner from one stage to another and there is a significant and observable arrest in the development, navigation through the later stages is going to be challenging. Likewise, relational issues throughout that person's life are going to result in failures and disappointments. If the individual has navigated successfully through these early stages of development, he is more likely to live a healthy and rewarding life until a trauma or significant stress hits his course. If the loss is too much and he is unable to cope, there is regression to an earlier stage of development. In regression, with help and treatment, recovery is faster and often complete.

3. **DEFENSE MECHANISMS:** Finally, operating defense mechanisms are listed with examples from the patient's life. There may be several defenses operating in one individual but for the sake of formulation it is good to highlight three or four important ones. Mature or immature, both types of defenses are worth mentioning as they show the strengths and weaknesses of

operating ego functions. Some people may have very conflicting defenses at the same time. With altruistic tendencies a person may exhibit sublimation, where he is able to channel energy to the betterment of other people; and with the death of a loved one he may show the defenses of denial and projection for a brief period of time. These immature defenses are not reflective of a person's operating system unless they are persistent and interfere with every relationship in his life.

B. OBJECT RELATIONS THEORY:

Object relations theory is an offshoot of psychoanalytic theory that emphasizes interpersonal relations, primarily in the family and especially between mother and child. *Object* is the significant person (*love object*) in someone's life that is the target of feelings or intentions. The quality of early life experiences shapes these internalized images of *love* objects and *self* which ultimately determines how the person is going to interact and relate to the rest of the world throughout his life span. Duration, quality, intensity and meaning of every significant relationship are explored in the dynamic assessment to make an assumption about the internalized *self* and *love* objects.

Splitting occurs when a person cannot keep two contradictory thoughts or feelings in mind at the same time, and therefore keeps the conflicting feelings apart and focuses on just one of them at a time.

Several writers have contributed in understanding this theory, including Melanie Kline, William Fairbairn, D. W. Winnicott, Henry Guntrip, Edith Jacobson and Margaret Mahler.

Margaret Mahler is famous for introducing the concept of "psychological birth" in a 3 month old child, who starts to sense itself as a separate individual and begins to remember. The mother provides a "holding space" for optimal growth.

From 6 months till 3 years of age, a child goes through four distinct phases of *Separation-individuation* state:

a. *Differentiation and body image*: Roughly from birth until 6 months of age, the child starts to learn more about his internal needs and is gradually willing to explore the environment. This stage also corresponds with his cognitive and psychomotor development along with his psychological growth.

b. *Practising period:* This period lasts from 6 months till 18 months of age. As he learns to sit up, crawl, stand up and walk, he starts to differentiate between himself and his mother and becomes increasingly more conscious of his body image and sense of self. He starts to take risks and immediately look for support and comfort from his primary care-taker.

c. *Rapprochement*: This phase lasts from 18 months until 3 years of age. The child enjoys and wants to share his development of greater autonomy. If growing in a supportive, caring, loving and encouraging environment, this phase is a time of the child enjoying greater self-reliance and a newfound ability to say "no". If a power struggle develops between the child and his parents, then it can become the "terrible twos".

d. *Object constancy:* Beyond the third year of life is the phase of object constancy. Hopefully by now the child has internalized the image of his mother/father and is able to carry that image when physically separated from the love object. The child is gradually getting comfortable in spending few hours a day away from his mother/father and is ready for pre-Kindergarten and later for regular school.

C. SELF-PSYCHOLOGY:

After the drive theory of ego psychology and the relational theory of object relations, Heinz Kohut made a case that in all this discussion of ego and object we forgot to pay attention to the *self*. He labeled his version of object relations theory "Self-Psychology" and placed his primary emphasis on *narcissism*. According to this theory, while the ego is developing through the psychosexual stages of development, the self is growing alongside on a parallel plane. Self-

Psychology emphasizes that narcissistic psychopathology is a result of parental lack of empathy during development. Consequently, the individual does not develop the full capacity to regulate self-esteem. As an adult, such an individual vacillates between an irrational over-estimation of the self and equally irrational feelings of inferiority. He relies on others for constant feedback to regulate his self-esteem and give him a sense of value. Kohut describes a certain aspect of narcissism inherent in all of us and he does not believe this type of narcissism to be pathological. He describes the self as "the center of the psychological universe" and believes we spend our entire lives trying to build and maintain our self-esteem. This healthy narcissism develops when *primary narcissistic needs* are met at an early age. When these needs are not met in certain patients, they search for gratification of missing childhood *self-object needs* in their adult lives. They also are fearful of encountering or repeating earlier past failures. As Dr. Jamie Mclean pointed out in his article "Psychotherapy with a Narcissistic Patient Using Kohut's Self Psychology Model", "These patients with pathological narcissism may present with an attitude of superiority or haughtiness, reflecting anxiety they feel over encountering further self-object failures. This fear may also manifest itself in relationships". The quality, intensity and duration of previous relationships help guide the clinician to make an assessment about individual's self-esteem and pathologic narcissistic needs.

Parents normally meet self-object needs of a child largely through two processes:

1. Mirroring Transference: When the parent reflects back to the child the feelings and thoughts the child is experiencing to give the child a sense of being validated and understood, it soothes the primary narcissistic needs of the child and helps him grow with a healthy self-esteem.

2. Idealizing Transference: When the parent accepts that the child wants to view the parent as his or her protector and feels a sense of strength and comfort from doing so, it is called *idealization*.

In therapy these two transferences merge while treating narcissistic patients and are collectively called *self-object transferences.*

RECOMMENDATIONS

Recommendations are written in the Bio-Psycho-Social format.

Biological Treatment: Detailed review of past and current medications and other biological treatments like Electro-Convulsive Therapy (ECT) or Trans-Magnetic Stimulation (TMS) helps guide the future treatment plan. Suggestions for medication change or dose alterations based on current research and evidence-based practices are discussed in this section.

Psychological   Treatment: Recommendations including mainly the suitability of the individual for dynamic therapy or supportive therapy are made here. After that determination, and when the person is found to be suitable for dynamic therapy, a decision is made about the type, frequency and intensity of therapy. Some patients may be suitable for Cognitive Behavioral Therapy in the beginning but later may graduate to more dynamic work.

Social Treatment: Housing, employment, hobbies, social networking, support groups, assisted living and much more, all fall under social interventions.

Transference and Countertransference issues:

It is very important for the therapist to foresee problems in future treatment. The psychological needs of both the therapist and the patient may cause problems and hinder the treatment. Knowing beforehand and getting prepared for those problems is a wise approach. A good formulation always contains a section where these issues are discussed in detail.

Prognosis:

Just writing "good", fair", or "guarded" is not enough. It is important to include a detailed discussion about the prognostic factors. Factors contributing to a good prognosis are as important as the factors pointing towards a guarded or poor prognosis. Lack of psychological mindedness, denial, non-compliance with treatment and resistance in general are considered poor prognostic factors; whereas good family support, permanent employment, ability to introspect and willingness to change are considered to be good prognostic factors.

Case Example (continued)
Psychodynamic Case Formulation
Identification:

Mrs. C is a 40 year-old Caucasian, married, female with past psychiatric history of Bipolar Disorder, Borderline Personality Disorder, Post-Traumatic Stress Disorder(PTSD), and remote history of alcohol dependence. She has had multiple hospitalizations mostly related to suicide attempts or plans to overdose on Tylenol.

DSM DIAGNOSIS:

Post-Traumatic Stress Disorder (PTSD)

Bipolar Disorder – most recent episode, depressed – stable on medications.

Borderline Personality Disorder
Alcohol use disorder, in sustained remission
Opioid use disorder, in sustained remission
Celiac Disease
Obesity

PREDISPOSING FACTORS Inherited/genetic:

There was no accurate history of psychiatric illness in her family but from patient's description of her mother, she appears to have had some problems with regulating her emotions and possibly a *personality disorder. Past records show a possible bipolar diagnosis in her mother reported by the patient which would genetically predispose her to the condition.*

Biologic/organic:

Her traumatic past with multiple sexual abuse and physical/verbal abuse by her mother also contributed to her mood dysregulation, PTSD and Borderline Personality Disorder. Patient has struggled with trials of multiple substances in high school, and alcohol when she was in her 20's presumably to self-medicate, which could have contributed further to her mood disorder.

Childhood events:

Patient's birth and infancy were clouded by her poor bond with her mother that predated with later knowledge of her mother wanting to abort her early in her pregnancy. She had equally poor relationships with her older sister as she felt she was being blamed for the divorce and a maternal grandmother who would call her "evil".

Most significant event of her childhood would be the death of her maternal grandfather. Increase in physical and emotional abuse by her mother following his death. Subsequent sexual trauma that began at age 10 with the therapist and having to give away her first born. And finally came the emancipation at age 16.

PRECIPITATING FACTORS:

Stressful job and her initial psychiatric breakdown around age 25.

PERPETUATING FACTORS:

Abusive marriages, strained relationships with her family, especially with her mother, were recurring themes in her multiple readmissions.

PROTECTIVE FACTORS:

She seeks comfort in her faith and has a supportive husband. She is able to utilize her skills via volunteering at a nursing home. She is open to treatment options including therapy, is very involved and compliant with her treatment and follow-ups. There is no ongoing substance abuse.

Dynamic Assessment

1. Ego psychology:

Psychosexual development:

Oral:

Since birth, patient was met by resistance from females in the family, including her mother, as they never held her at birth. Patient's introduction to the oral stage, where the mouth is the source of libidinal gratification, was met with denial of being breast fed. She lacked the nurturing emotional bond with her mother, who is reported to have contemplated aborting patient early in the pregnancy.

Without having been breast-fed, patient also did not experience the important event of the weaning process, which allows the infant to experience self-awareness, that he/she does not control the environment, and thereby learns of delayed *gratification which in turn lays the ground work for capacity for independence and trust.*

Although she received nurturing care from her grandfather, which could have offset some of the damage done by lack of it from her mother, she appears to have longed for her mother's attention which was given to her sister, as she often reverts back to the lack of emotional investment in her as a child and growing up. Both the neglect by her mother and overprotection by her grandfather seem to have played a part in the patient's arrest in this stage. This is apparent in the patient's maladapted personality issues and her dependence on others to fulfill her poor sense of self. It also can be inferred that her substance-abuse issues and need for immediate gratification have their roots in being fixated in this stage.

Anal:

There are no apparent anal-retentive behaviors besides the eating disorder that the patient struggles with. She may have had a lax toilet training as opposed to a traumatic one. Some maladaptation in this stage is evident in her rebellious and boundary-pushing behavior with her mother in her later years.

Phallic:

Successful navigation of this stage is dependent on the resolution of the Oedipus/Electra complex, wherein the child through the resolution of the id-ego conflict, internalizes mortality and chooses to comply with societal rules. If this conflict with the opposite-sex parent is unresolved, a phallic-stage fixation arises, which could result in a girl becoming an adult who strives to dominate men or becomes an unusually seductive or submissive woman.

Mrs. C's continued identification with her grandfather/father-figure instead of her mother, and his demise prior to the resolution of this stage, could have been a precipitant of her fixation in this stage, as it did not allow her to reach the point of identification with her mother and resolution of competing for his love. Her relationships with usually older males and her current husband who she in a Freudian slip refers to as "father" provides some proof of the same. Her poor self-esteem has manifested itself in her submissive nature during her two past marriages where she continually suffered physical abuse and during continued emotional abuse by her mother.

Latency:

Following the death of the patient's grandfather and traumatic abuse by her therapist, this phase was marked by lack of interest in academics, no clear set of friends, substance abuse, delinquent behavior such as running away from home, skipping school etc. which would relate with Anna Freud's thought of the consequences of delayed Oedipal resolution that follows into this stage. However, the patient was also attempting to navigate this phase by identifying with Arts instead of Academics. She actively participated in cheerleading, a trumpet band etc., exercising her libidinal drives externally.

Genital:

Maturation in terms of capacity to love and work are hallmarks of this stage which starts at puberty and continues into adulthood.

The patient's foundation laid by arrests and fixations in past stages definitely makes it difficult to successfully navigate this stage, although she has found "unconditional love" in her current husband. Although she did very well in the structured setting of the military, she was unable to function on her own after discharge, and has been unemployed since that time.

Structural Model:

The patient's impulsive suicidal attempts in response to negative situations, along with her struggles with substance abuse as a form of instant gratification, imply that she operates on the level of Id. Her high moral values taught by her grandfather and her attempts to practice them also shows a fair development of the Super-ego in her early years. However, her weak ego development is evident in her utilizing several defense mechanisms including regression at times when there is anxiety, and presumed thoughts of ill-will towards herself.

Defense mechanism:

Mrs. C utilizes multiple defense mechanisms, some mature and others immature. Most prominent among them is **splitting**, where she categorizes people with whom she has had a good relationship and others who have been destructive. For example, she describes her mother as "evil" and has nothing but praise for her *grandfather. She appears to see people who remind her of her mother as negative as noted by her constant conflict with her therapist in Denver. She likely was reliving her arguments and conflicts with her mother that eventually led to her closing off from the therapist. **Regression** is also evident, with her physical gestures, and general child-like presentation. She also uses **humor** intermittently along with **intellectualization**. Use of **anticipation**, defined as committing oneself to the needs of others over and above one's own needs, is also noted in the patient as she fails to draw boundaries on the limits of her volunteering abilities, taking on more than she is able to do and then struggling with anxiety and poor sleep. She was possibly also using **suppression** in her early twenties via alcohol abuse.*

2. Object relations

The object relations theory is the process by which the psyche (the conscious and unconscious) develops in relation to others during childhood. It also suggests that how a person relates to others and situations in adulthood are shaped by their experiences in infancy.

The patient, having met with emotional neglect from her mother, was unable to integrate the good and bad representations of the love-object (her mother), which usually occurs between age 1-3. Secondary to the failure of the integration she has maintained the split in internal organization which is now seen in her borderline personality. Patient is arrested in the paranoid-schizoid position.

Patient's interactions are not processed objectively but rather through her internal representations and corresponding actions, which in turn often provoke the reaction that is expected by the internal system (projective identification). This is further reinforces the behavior. This can be seen in her aggression and conflict with her providers in the past.

3. Self-Psychology

As Heinz Kohut stated, "the development of the self requires the integration of two major spheres i.e. the grandiose self and the idealized parental image – collectively, represents the bi-polar self".

Development of narcissism is facilitated by creation of self-object, usually a parent, which represents person's self-organization. This self-object mirrors the child's self-state by providing an empathic relationship and maintaining internal emotional vulnerabilities. Faults arise when empathic failure by self-objects prevents the integration of the spheres, but it can be compensated for by idealized self-object image. This is true in patient's case where she was neglected by her mother and the self-object was transferred to her grandfather. Also her substance abuse issues and alcohol dependence in the past can be explained as failure to obtain a basic sense of adequacy, self-worth, dignity, respect and well-being from caregivers.

Cognitive Distortions

Dr. K. Sohail/Dr. Rizwan Ali

Some of cognitive distortions that are apparent in patient from her history are overgeneralization, jumping to conclusions, dichotomous thinking.

Countertransference/Transference Issues

Only countertransference that noticeably occurred intermittently was the
questioning of whether narration of the numerous traumatic events in the patient life was real, given the knowledge of patient's history of factitious disorder.

Recommendations
Biological

Patient is on multiple medications for depression, mood stabilization, anxiety and PTSD symptoms. At present will continue on Escitalopram, lamotrigine, lithium, mirtazapine, prazosin, diazepam, with intent to address poly-pharmacy later and will try to simplify her medication regimen.

Labs such as TSH, lithium level, BMP to be monitored periodically when indicated.

Encourage sleep hygiene along with proper diet and exercise.

Psychological

Patient is already attending Dialectal Behavioral Therapy (DBT) and is at the verge of completion. Will attempt to reintroduce DBT skills at intervals to refresh her mindfulness, psychosocial skills etc.

Continue to provide supportive therapy as needed with good limit setting to prevent over dependence.

<u>Social</u>

She volunteers at a nursing home in attempt to keep herself occupied.

Prognosis

Fair at present with adherence to treatment and follow-ups. She may have difficulty dealing with the death of her supportive older husband in the future, given her unshakable reliance on him and lack of any other support in the community.

CONCLUSION:

Psychodynamic formulation is a very important and unique document which reflects upon the person's upbringing, psychological development, struggles, navigation through different stressful life events, strengths and weaknesses; it might have been the very first attempt to understand the person in a purely empathic manner with keen interest and background knowledge. This document not only helps the clinician with the treatment plan but also can be used as a guiding tool to measure progress. The formulation should be considered a living document which changes every day and should be updated regularly depending on the person's progress in treatment.

SECTION THREE

ABOUT THE AUTHORS

Chapter Twelve

WHEN A DREAM COMES TRUE
BY
DR. K. SOHAIL

Every day when I go to my clinic to see my patients, I have a sense of gratitude. I love the work I do. That is why I say that I never worked in my life, even for one day.

When I was a young man I used to dream of becoming a psychotherapist and having my own psychotherapy clinic where I could see my patients and their family members. My Green Zone Clinic is my dream come true.

Now that I reflect on my professional journey I can look back on some significant milestones. Let me share some of those milestones in this essay,

MY MOTHER'S DREAM

My mother Aisha had a dream. She wanted me to become a doctor. When I asked her why, she told me that I had been born with a congenital anomaly--a part of my left ear lobe was missing. She used to feel so embarrassed that she kept it covered with a scarf.

When I was three years old, she took me to see a surgeon who performed an operation to correct the deformity. My mother was so impressed by that surgeon that she told him, "I would like my son Sohail to become a doctor like you." I am sure the surgeon was quite pleased to hear that comment.

MY FATHER'S ILLNESS

When I was ten years old, my father Basit had a breakdown. I remember seeing him talking to the stars at night and standing in one spot for hours in a catatonic state during the day. He would drink dozens of glasses of water daily, necessitating frequent trips to the bathroom. My mother took him to see a doctor, an internist, a psychiatrist and a spiritual healer. He even received shock treatment, but nothing worked. After a year of this, just as he had become mysteriously sick, he mysteriously recovered. After his recovery, this agnostic mathematician became a deeply religious man. He started wearing very modest clothes, eating plain food and leading a simple life. He became a mystic, a *sufi*. His family and friends thought he had suffered a nervous breakdown, while he believed he had experienced a spiritual breakthrough. I think my father's illness must have unconsciously inspired me to become a psychotherapist.

FATHER RECOVERED, MOTHER BECAME ILL

When my father recovered from his illness, he left his teaching job in Government College Kohat and took a position in a Cantonment Board High School in Peshawar for half the salary. My mother was so distressed by his illness that she developed thyrotoxicosis [hyperactivity of the thyroid gland], for which she was treated with radio-active iodine. Rather than getting better, she got worse. I remember the night when she slipped into a coma and we thought she was going to die. When we took her to the hospital the next morning, we learned that she was suffering from myxedema [hypo-activity of the thyroid gland] because she had been given an overdose of radio-active iodine. For her myxedema she had to take thyroxin for the rest of her life.

Later on she developed arthritis for which a specialist prescribed steroids. Since she could not afford to see the specialist on a regular basis, she continued to take steroids without appropriate follow-up and developed complications — diabetes and hypertension. She could not consume sugar because of her diabetes and had to limit her salt intake because of her high blood pressure.

As a young man, I watched her suffer for years. It was heartbreaking.

I think that seeing both of my parents suffering helped me develop compassion for people with mental and physical illnesses.

Since my mother could not afford to see a specialist, I became a believer in universal health care for both the *haves* and the *have nots*. I came to believe that it is the responsibility of the state to provide free health care for all citizens. That is one reason that I practice in Canada rather than America; I feel proud that Canada has a universal health care system and find it sad that in America, one of the richest countries in the world, millions of men, women and children lack health care insurance.

SIGMUND FREUD AND PSYCHOANALYSIS

When I was a teenager I loved visiting libraries and reading books. Like the Argentinian writer Victor Borges, I believed that paradise was not a garden but a library. In the libraries I used to visit the literature, religion, psychology and philosophy sections. In a few years I must have read hundreds of books. Then one day, unexpectedly, I stumbled upon a thousand-page book on Sigmund Freud and psychoanalysis. It was a goldmine. After reading that book I fell in love with Freud. That book inspired me to become a psychotherapist. Like Freud, I wanted to explore the mysteries of the mind and help people with emotional problems. In later years, I was impressed by many other psychologists, psychotherapists and philosophers, but Freud always remained my first love.

APPLYING TO KHYBER MEDICAL COLLEGE

When I passed Grade Twelve with honors, I applied to the Khyber Medical College in Peshawar. In spite of being on the merit list, I was rejected because my parents did not have a Peshawar domicile certificate as they had migrated from India in 1947. I told the authorities that I had lived in that province my whole life, but in their eyes, that was not good enough. All of my friends who had lower marks than I were accepted but I was not. I felt sad and dejected. My dream of becoming a doctor was shattered.

To cope with my depression, I went to see my Grandmother Sarwar in Lahore. A few days later, while I was visiting my Uncle Alla-ud-din, I met his lawyer friend, whom I called Uncle Saeed. He was always very affectionate towards me. When he asked me how I was doing, I told him that in spite of getting very good marks, I was refused admission because of not having a domicile certificate.

Uncle Saeed asked me to come to his office. When I went to see him the next day, he listened to my story and wrote a long letter representing me as a lawyer. He sent copies of the letter to the principal of the Medical College, the vice-chancellor of Peshawar University and the governor of the province. Luckily, Air Marshal Asghar Khan, the governor at that time, was very sympathetic to students' causes. He set up a special committee to investigate the case. The committee interviewed my father and within a short time I was accepted into the Khyber Medical College. That was in January 1970, three months after my friends had started their classes. At the end of 1974 when I passed my final examination with flying colors, my mother was ecstatic as her dream had come true.

MEETING DR. AHMED ALI

When I learned that there was no internship program available in our university for specialization in psychiatry, I went looking for a psychiatrist in town. I walked all over the city of Peshawar for three days before I found Dr. Ahmed Ali's psychiatric clinic. I went inside and introduced myself. I told Dr. Ali, "I have graduated from the Medical College and I am free for the next three months. I have a dream of becoming a psychiatrist and having a clinic like yours one day. Can you help me?" Dr. Ali was very gracious. He brought in a special chair and asked me to sit next to him. For the next three months I saw the patients with him. He not only discussed those patients with me but also gave me textbooks to read. At the end of the three months when he went to his village for a week, he asked me to sit in his chair and see his patients in his absence. I felt honored. Those three months of training and one week of independent practice gave me a lot of confidence. After that experience

I was convinced that I could become a psychiatrist and have my own clinic one day.

DOING MY INTERNSHIP

After summer vacation, since I could not apply to psychiatry for an internship, I applied to the Department of Gynecology and Obstetrics. I remember being invited by the administrator of the Lady Reading Hospital Peshawar for an interview. When I saw him he said,

"Are you Dr. Sohail?"

"Yes, I am." I responded.

"You have applied to do an internship in the Gynecology and Obstetrics Department?"

"Yes, I have."

"Do you know that in the last seventy-five years there has been no male house officer in the labor room?"

"Does that mean there will be no male house officer for the next seventy-five years?"

"Do not get upset, Dr. Sohail. I am just warning you that Pukhtoon women are very traditional, religious and conservative. They do not want to be examined by male doctors."

"I will take my chances." I responded.

During the selection interviews I was lucky that Dr. Shamim Majeed accepted me and I started my internship in the labor room. During the first week Dr. Majeed asked the Head Nurse, Falak Naz, to help me integrate into the unit. She was very helpful and supportive to me. Whenever a female patient was reluctant to be examined by the male doctor she said in a reassuring voice, *"doctor day, saray na day"* [He is a doctor, not a man]. She had magic in her words. It worked each time.

When Dr. Majeed discovered that I had a special interest in psychiatry, she asked me to see those patients who suffered from anxiety and panic disorder, especially post-partum depression. She was a wonderful professor. I learnt a lot from her.

WORKING IN IRAN

After finishing my internship on the Gynecology/Obstetrics ward and the Medical Ward, I went to Iran for two years to work and save money for my post-graduate studies. From the window of my clinic in a children's hospital in Hamadan, I could see the tomb of the famous physician Ibn Sina (known as Avicenna in the Western world), a great inspiration for me. Over the year that I worked in that clinic, I saw patients all day and during the evening wrote letters to universities all over the world, as I hoped to pursue residency training in psychiatry. I must have sent hundreds of letters. After nine months of this, I received good news. I was accepted by psychiatry departments in Ireland, New Zealand and Newfoundland. I consulted Dr. Shamim Majeed and she suggested I go to Canada because a Canadian Fellowship was well-respected all over the world.

COMING TO CANADA

Thus in October 1977, I came to Canada and joined Memorial University of Newfoundland. Dr. John Hoenig was the chairman of the Department of Psychiatry at the time. One day I said to him, "I want to thank you for accepting me in your residency program, but I am curious as to why you accepted me, as you had never interviewed me." Dr. Hoenig smiled and said, "All three of your references stated that you were a good poet and I thought if you were a good poet, you would also be a good psychiatrist." Dr. Hoenig's wife was an artist, and he had a great respect for both writers and artists. He was an admirer of phenomenologist Karl Jaspers and had translated his book into English.

During my residency training I had an opportunity to learn the art and science of psychotherapy. I had the privilege of working with wonderful teachers like Dr. Kotsopoulous, Dr. Liberakis, Dr. James and Dr. Wolf. Dr. Eugene Wolf took me under his wing and groomed me as a psychotherapist. He was much influenced by the work of Harry Stack Sullivan and introduced me to Sullivanian philosophy.

To broaden my philosophical horizons and study different schools of psychology, I not only read the books and papers of leading philosophers, psychologists and psychotherapists, but also went to seminars and conferences to listen to scholars like Peter Sifneos, Murray Bowen and Victor Frankl. I wanted to learn from their knowledge, experience and wisdom and incorporate their ideas into my own philosophy and clinical practice.

CREATING A GREEN ZONE CLINIC

After working in general and psychiatric hospitals in Newfoundland, New Brunswick and Ontario, I decided to open my own clinic. In 1995 Anne Henderson and I started the Creative Psychotherapy Clinic. Later we were joined by Bette Davis from Newfoundland as a co-therapist. With the help of my two co-therapists and my patients I discovered the Green Zone Philosophy, the basis of the Green Zone Therapy that we offer in our clinic. Over the years hundreds of patients and their families have benefited from that program. It helped them create a healthy, happy and peaceful lifestyle, that we call Green Zone Living. We get so many referrals from doctors, nurses and social workers that we have a one-year waiting list. To help our patients we have written a series of Green Zone Books, produced videos and created a website. Many patients visit our website and read our books while they are on the waiting list. It is so rewarding to work with well-motivated patients who are inspired to change their lifestyle for the better. No wonder I look forward to going to work every day. For me serving my community and humanity is a great honor. That is why I consider my Green Zone Clinic my dream come true.

Psychotherapy transforms breakdowns into breakthroughs – Dr. K. Sohail

---

Chapter Thirteen

FINDING MY PASSION
BY
DR. RIZWAN ALI

BACKGROUND:

I grew up in a humble household in the suburbs of Karachi, Pakistan. My father was an instructor of metallurgy in a nuclear power plant, and my mother taught mathematics to eighth and ninth graders in a girls' high school. Both of them also tutored neighborhood kids in the evening. They were very hard-working and were very well-respected in the community because of their manners, love of education and passion for teaching. They were very young when they immigrated to Pakistan from Hyderabad, India in the late 1950's – just a few years after the partition of India. They didn't have many resources or much education. My father worked during the daytime and studied for his degree in engineering in the evenings. My mother started working as a teacher right after my birth, to support the family. I was their only child for the first eight years of my life. Later on, four sisters arrived, one after another.

After the fifth grade my uncle Mr. S. G. Husseini, who was the Wing Commander in the Pakistani Air Force, took me under his wings. He was a very learned man who could speak several languages, and was an avid reader and a prolific writer and poet. He had a library in his house which always attracted me, and I started spending a lot of time in his library from an early age. He had books on literature, philosophy, sociology, arts, humanities, economics, and many other diverse topics. When I was only fifteen years old and in the tenth grade, I read his copy of *The Interpretation of Dreams* by Sigmund Freud. He would take me to visit his literary friends and to poetry recitals and musical programs, and would encourage me to participate in debate competitions at the very highest level. I won a few trophies and he would introduce me to his friends with pride: "Meet my nephew, he won the extemporary debate competition recently".

My uncle was the one who made sure that I went to the best schools in the city. He, and not my parents, went with me for the admission process and or any parent-teacher meetings. He was my guardian, mentor and god-father.

CONCRETIZATION OF A DREAM:

I remember that when I was eight years old my father took me to a tailor's shop with his old suit and asked him to alter it to my size. I felt very proud wearing that suit with my father's necktie. In those days you would go to a photo studio for a picture on special occasions. I went to a studio with my father and posed for a perfect picture, which I still have. When the picture was framed my parents insisted that the bottom part of the picture should have a blank white strip where they asked the photographer to write, *"Dr. Rizwan Ali"*. So at age eight my parents decided for me that I should be a doctor and my task was to live up to their dream and my uncle Mr. Husseini made sure in a most kind and caring way that I achieved it. I studied hard so that my name was on the merit list of the best medical school in Karachi, the Dow Medical College, which is now the Dow University of Health Sciences.

EXPLORING THE WORLD:

Until medical school, I was a very studious person – something like a nerd. I had written and staged plays with the neighborhood kids, but my favorite pastime was to climb up a mango tree in my backyard and read books – novels, poetry and short stories. In the eleventh grade, I started writing poetry and edited the magazine of my college. Other than that I was a shy, introverted type of person, who had a very limited circle of friends and didn't know much about the outside world. It was in medical school that I started to expand my wings and explore the world around me. My training in debates came handy, and I was one of the best debaters during those days. I had the privilege of first-hand meetings with some of the legendary writers and poets of those times, like Ahmad Faraz and Ubaidullah Aleem. Poetry recitals and musical sittings were a must during the weekends in those days. Long, unending discussions over a cup of tea on politics, literature, music and life in general were the fuel of my life. Along with medical school I was actively involved in so many other things in addition to medical school that it is hard for me to believe now.

THEATER AND MUSIC:

During my final year of medical school, one of my friends introduced me to Mussadiq Sanwal. After my uncle in my childhood, Mussadiq has had the greatest influence on my life. He came from Lahore and settled in Karachi. With him and a few other friends, I started a theater group called *Baang* (the sound of a rooster's crowing in the morning – signifying a wake-up call for society). That group became a great success and the talk of the town within a couple of years. We staged several high-profile plays related to mental health, women's rights and the conservation of nature, in collaboration with international organizations like WWF, UNICEF and IUCN. We received rave reviews in the country's leading newspapers and magazines.

I started my formal music lessons during those times as well. I studied tabla (an Indian percussion instrument) for two years and played some with friends whenever they sang.

PEDIATRICS:

After my graduation from medical school I had to choose between pediatrics and psychiatry. Pediatrics was my first choice, because it was culturally accepted to be a pediatrician, and I loved children and they were very comfortable around me as well. During my house-job (internship) at Civil Hospital Karachi, I realized that this was not the right field for me, because I would get attached to the children I was treating and couldn't bear to see them suffer or die. I was working in a big tertiary-care hospital in those days and children were coming in with all sorts of serious illnesses. Some of them were not lucky enough to make it, and I used to get very sad and upset and sometimes cry if any child passed away. My seniors suggested that I try some other field, because in pediatrics it was inevitable that I would deal with children with ailments that some them might not survive.

FINDING PSYCHIATRY – MY TRUE PASSION:

By the end of my internship, there was an entrance test for psychiatry post-graduate training at Jinnah Post-graduate Medical Center (JPMC). I passed that exam with distinction without any preparation or formal training in psychiatry. My success at that test told me at once that I had found my field. My friends used to confide in me and always complimented me that I was a good listener, even before I started my formal training in psychiatry. Dr. Haroon Ahmad was my teacher and supervisor at JPMC. It was 1990, almost 26 years ago, when I started psychiatry, and there has not been a single day when I regretted my decision.

I look forward to seeing my patients and feel great when I see improvement in their mood, behavior and overall lives. After further studies and exams, I moved to the US in 1994 and started my psychiatry residency in Richmond at Virginia Commonwealth University/Medical College of Virginia. Dr. Norman Camp, who was then the president of the Virginia Psychoanalytic Society, was my supervisor. He helped me hone my passion for psychotherapy and psychodynamics at that time and for the years to come.

After my residency I worked for almost ten years for a state out-patient mental health clinic in under-served areas of Virginia. During those years, I had my private practice in Roanoke along with my full-time job. I was able to practice supportive psychotherapy, and with a very few selected patients, dynamic psychotherapy. In 2005, after much consideration, I finally decided to go into academic psychiatry, and started working at the Veterans Affairs Medical Center in Salem, Virginia. Here, with the Virginia Tech Carilion School of Medicine, we have an active psychiatry residency program, and I started teaching psychotherapy and psychodynamic formulation to senior residents. I supervise, hold lectures and do seminars for the medical students and residents throughout the year.

PSYCHIATRIST AS A RESERVOIR:

I tell my students that a psychiatrist is like a reservoir: he goes to work in the morning and distributes the water to all of his patients through multiple faucets all around him. By the evening, he is drained and exhausted. It is very important for him to take care of himself and to make sure that the reservoir gets filled up every day with love, care, and compassion. Therefore, spending time with friends and family, giving time to myself, reading, writing, and listening to music, having a hobby, going for a walk, and in general living a rich and nurturing life is very important for me. I am married to Fouzia, and we have two beautiful and intelligent daughters, Marvi and Maha.

I have been actively involved in the Psychiatric Society of Virginia for more than a decade and have served in different capacities, including the presidency of this august organization; I am now representing Virginia in the American Psychiatric Association Assembly. I also preside over two musical groups in the area and volunteer my time helping our community theater with lights, sound, and set design and construction.

My main inspiration to write this book with Dr. Khalid Sohail came when I translated poems written in Urdu by a renowned poetess, Dr. Sarwat Zahra, which revived my confidence in writing in general, after a very long time.

I love to hike, travel, read, play the harmonium and sing—all because I want to keep my reservoir full, so that I may continue helping my patients who are already in pain and distress.

Becoming a Psychotherapist